Quick & Ea

Hot and Spicy

p

Contents

Introduction

Changing tastes and a more daring approach to what we eat have led in recent years to a growing interest in food from many different cultures. Among the most popular cuisines are those from China, India, Thailand, Mexico – anywhere, in fact, that serves hot and spicy dishes, bursting with new and exciting flavours that sometimes make your eyes water, as well as your mouth. Soups, fish, meat, chicken and vegetables are transformed with the addition of fresh chillies, ginger and garlic and with a range of dried spices. The recipes in this book are quick and easy to make, but still impressive – you can create something really special for a supper party, and you can even top it off with a hot and spicy desert.

Store-cupboard items

In the countries from which these recipes are taken, most of the ingredients are bought absolutely fresh from the daily markets. In Thailand the diet is mostly based on fish – caught, landed and sold within a very short time. Vegetables are also carefully chosen and purchased daily.

However, there are some items that can be kept on hand. Rice is the most important staple food, either forming the basis of the main dish or, more often, served as a side dish, perhaps with herbs, spices or vegetables added. Long-grain white rice and Indian basmati rice with its distinctive aroma and flavour are staples and readily available in supermarkets. They will keep for quite a while stored in an airtight container. Noodles are another staple, used frequently in Chinese and Thai cookery where they are tossed in a wok with meat or fish and vegetables, and seasoned generously. They come in many forms and among the most popular are rice noodles, almost transparent and shaped as flat ribbons or thin vermicelli, and the egg noodles favoured by the Chinese, a rich yellow in colour and crinkled in shape. Both types are not so much cooked as softened by soaking in boiling water for just a few minutes.

A range of oils is also useful, and some of these will already be kept in the average storecupboard for general use. Sunflower oil and vegetable oil are the most widely used, because they are light and mild, complementing the food rather than flavouring it. Olive oil is

commonly used in some cuisines, notably Mexican, And it is best to choose a really good virgin olive oil. It is also worth investing in a bottle of sesame oil made from roasted sesame seeds and full of flavour. This is not used for cooking food because it burns easily. Instead, it is drizzled over the finished dish. And for the very brave, a bottle of chilli oil is hot stuff indeed.

Beans are often used as the basis of spicy dishes because they readily absorb the delicious flavours of the dish. The classic is the ever-popular Mexican chilli-bean stew, warming and filling. When using beans you have two options: you can buy packets of dried beans, which are very cheap and keep well, but have to be soaked overnight before cooking; or you can buy cans of ready-cooked beans which are a little more expensive but really useful if you want to rustle up a quick dish for lunch or supper.

Also readily available, and ideal for anyone with limited spare time are the jars of sauces and pastes stocked by supermarkets everywhere. Using bottled sauces is not quite the same as making them from scratch, but they still taste good. Green and red Thai curry pastes can be used to whip up a green fish curry or a red lamb curry. Indian curry pastes range from mild to seriously hot. Many of the recipes in this book need dried spices, such as cumin, coriander, cardamom and

turmeric. Their flavour deteriorates rapidly, so unless you are planning to do a lot of this type of cooking buy them in small quantities and store them in a cool, dark place. Add some authentic seasoning sauces to your store-cupboard - soy sauce, made from fermented soya beans and Thai fish sauce, made from salted fermented fish.

Chillies, Ginger and Garlic

All these items add a real zing to your hot and spicy cookery, but it is fair to say that when it comes to heat, chillies are the star. There are many varieties of chilli, and different cultures favour different ones, so it is worth looking out for the right one for a particular dish. Many recipes call for fresh chillies, but dried crushed chillies may be substituted. Some chillies are quite mild, while others are fiery hot – larger chillies are usually milder than small ones, and red chillies tend to be a little sweeter and milder than green ones. If you are in any doubt about eating a dish seasoned with chillies, remember that most of the heat is in the seeds, so you should remove these before cooking.

Thai dishes often include 'bird-eye' chillies. These are small and either red or green, and are very, very hot. In Mexico, where chillies of one sort or another are included in virtually every recipe, the small green variety called jalapeño is especially popular, and dried chillies – ancho and chipotle – are also used.

Chillies are incredibly irritating to the skin, so if you are particularly sensitive, wear rubber gloves when preparing them, and if you are removing the seeds, do so with the point of a sharp knife. Always wash your hands really thoroughly afterwards, and make sure you keep your hands away from your eyes.

Fresh ginger is a wonderful spice, adding flavour as well as fire. Substituting the dried powdered ginger used in baking is out of the question. The fresh or 'green' root is sold in supermarkets everywhere, however, and your only problem may be identifying it. It is quite small and very knobbly, not unlike a Jerusalem artichoke in shape and colour, and it should feel firm to the touch. When

the root is peeled, the yellow flesh is revealed and the delicious aroma wafts out. Ginger is usually grated and thrown into the wok at the start of cooking a stir-fry, infusing the oil with its fantastic flavour.

Garlic, crushed or chopped, is used throughout the world, and not just for spicy cookery. Again, garlic is easy to come by, the individual cloves packed tightly together to form a bulb. Garlic's reputation for tainting the breath is unfortunately quite valid, but the special flavour and subtle kick it imparts is worth it – chasing it down with parsley or caraway seeds is said to help.

Cooking Utensils

There is no essential piece of equipment needed for hot and spicy cuisine – your usual saucepans and a good heavy frying pan will be absolutely fine – but if you intend to do a lot of spicy cooking, a wok is a very useful item of equipment to have in the kitchen. The wok is shallow and convex in shape, allowing the heat to spread evenly, especially if it sits on a 'collar' over the heat source. It is an ideal pan for stir-frying because the curved sides make it easy to toss food as it cooks. For this you need a spatula with a long wooden handle to insulate your hand from the heat. Although they are pricey, it is worth

investing in a cast-iron wok, as these are most effective at retaining heat - and fast cooking is the key to successful stir-frying.

The wok is at its best when it is well seasoned – to do this, it should be wiped inside and out with oil, and brought up to a high temperature either in the oven or on the hob. This process is repeated a few times to give a good coating. The seasoned wok will then only need to be wiped out after use, although it can be cleaned with soap and water and dried immediately to prevent rusting.

KEY	
	Simplicity level 1 – 3 (1 easiest, 3 slightly harder)
	Preparation time
	Cooking time

Spicy Gazpacho

This classic Spanish cold soup is given a Mexican twist by adding chillies and fresh coriander. Serve with chunks of bread.

NUTRITIONAL INFORMATION

Calories . . . . . . .125 Sugars 10g
Protein . . . . .3g   Fat 8g
Carbohydrate . . . .11g Saturates 1g

30 mins, plus 2–3 hrs chilling   0 mins

SERVES 4–6

I N G R E D I E N T S

1 cucumber

2 green peppers

6 ripe flavourful tomatoes

½ fresh hot chilli

½–1 onion, finely chopped

3–4 garlic cloves, chopped

4 tbsp extra-virgin olive oil

¼–½ tsp ground cumin

2–4 tsp sherry vinegar, or a combination of balsamic vinegar and wine vinegar

4 tbsp chopped fresh coriander

2 tbsp chopped fresh parsley

300 ml/10 fl oz cold vegetable or chicken stock

600 ml/1 pint tomato juice or canned crushed tomatoes

salt and pepper

ice cubes, to serve

water. Slide off the skins, cut in half, deseed if wished, and chop. Carefully deseed the chilli, then chop it finely.

3 Combine half the cucumber, green pepper, tomatoes and onion in a blender or a food processor with all the chilli, garlic, olive oil, cumin, vinegar, coriander and parsley. Process with enough stock for a smooth purée.

4 Pour the puréed soup into a bowl and stir in the remaining stock and tomato juice. Add the remaining green pepper, cucumber, tomatoes and onion, stirring well. Season with salt and pepper to taste, then cover the bowl with cling film and chill for 2–3 hours.

5 Ladle into bowls and serve with ice cubes in each bowl.

1 Cut the cucumber in quarters lengthways, remove the seeds and dice the flesh. Cut the peppers in half and dice them after removing cores and seeds.

2 Skin the tomatoes: place in a bowl, cover with boiling water and stand for 30 seconds. Drain and plunge into cold

Mexican Chilli Soup

This soup evolved from the food stalls that line the streets of Tlalpan, a suburb of Mexico City: avocado, chicken and smoky chipotle chillies.

NUTRITIONAL INFORMATION

Calories 218	Sugars 1g	
Protein 28g	Fat 11g	
Carbohydrate 2g	Saturates 2g	

 15 mins   0 mins

SERVES 4

I N G R E D I E N T S

1.5 litres/2¾ pints chicken stock

2–3 garlic cloves, finely chopped

1–2 chipotle chillies, cut into very thin strips (see Cook's Tip)

1 avocado

lime or lemon juice, for tossing

3–5 spring onions, thinly sliced

350–400 g/12–14 oz cooked chicken breast meat, torn or cut into shreds or thin strips

2 tbsp chopped fresh coriander

TO SERVE

1 lime, cut into wedges

handful of tortilla chips (optional)

1 Place the stock in a pan with the garlic and chipotle chillies and bring to the boil.

2 Cut the avocado in half around the stone. Twist apart, then remove the stone with a knife. Carefully peel off the skin, dice the flesh and toss gently in lime or lemon juice to prevent discoloration.

3 Arrange the prepared spring onions, chicken, avocado and fresh coriander in the base of 4 soup bowls or in a large serving bowl.

4 Ladle hot stock over the ingredients in the soup bowls, and serve the soup with wedges of lime and a handful of tortilla chips if using.

COOK'S TIP
Chipotle chillies are smoked and dried jalapeño chillies and are available canned or dried. They add a distinctive smoky flavour to dishes.

Authentic Guacamole

Guacamole is at its best when it is freshly made. Serve it as a sauce for anything Mexican, or as a dip for raw vegetable sticks or tortilla chips.

NUTRITIONAL INFORMATION

Calories 212	Sugars 1g	
Protein 2g	Fat 21g	
Carbohydrate 3g	Saturates 4g	

 15 mins   0 mins

SERVES 4

I N G R E D I E N T S

1 ripe tomato

2 limes

2–3 ripe small to medium avocados, or 1–2 large ones

¼–½ onion, finely chopped

pinch of ground cumin

pinch of mild chilli powder

½–1 fresh green chilli, such as jalapeño or serrano, deseeded and finely chopped

1 tbsp finely chopped fresh coriander leaves, plus extra for garnishing

salt (optional)

tortilla chips, to serve (optional)

1 Place the tomato in a bowl, cover it with boiling water and leave it to stand for 30 seconds. Drain and plunge the tomato into cold water. The skin will then slide off easily. Cut in half, deseed and chop the flesh.

2 Squeeze the juice from the limes into a small bowl. Cut one avocado in half around the stone. Twist apart, then remove the stone with a knife. Carefully peel off the skin, dice the flesh and toss in the bowl of lime juice to prevent the flesh discolouring. Mash coarsely.

3 Add the onion, tomato, cumin, chilli powder, chopped chilli and fresh coriander to the avocados. If the dish is to be used as a dip for tortilla chips, do not add salt. If it is to be used as a sauce, add salt to taste.

4 To serve the Guacamole as a dip, transfer it to a serving dish, garnish with finely chopped fresh coriander and serve with tortilla chips.

COOK'S TIP

Avocados grow in abundance in Mexico, and Guacamole is used to add richness and flavour to all manner of dishes. Try spooning it into soups, especially chicken or seafood, or spreading it into sandwiches on thick crusty rolls.

Hot & Sour Soup

Hot-and-sour mixtures are popular throughout the East, especially in Thailand. This soup typically has either prawns or chicken added.

NUTRITIONAL INFORMATION

Calories	71	Sugars	.......0.1g
Protein	.........8g	Fat	..........4g
Carbohydrate	....1g	Saturates	....0.1g

30 mins 25 mins

SERVES 4

INGREDIENTS

350 g/12 oz whole raw or cooked prawns in shells

1 tbsp vegetable oil

1 lemon grass stalk, roughly chopped

2 kaffir lime leaves, shredded

1 green chilli, deseeded and chopped

1.2 litres/2 pints chicken or fish stock

1 lime

1 tbsp Thai fish sauce

1 red bird-eye chilli, deseeded and thinly sliced

1 spring onion, thinly sliced

salt and pepper

1 tbsp finely chopped coriander

1 Peel the prawns and reserve the shells. Devein them, cover and chill.

2 Heat the oil in a large pan and stir-fry the prawn shells for 3–4 minutes until they turn pink. Add the lemon grass, lime leaves, green chilli and stock. Grate the zest from the lime and add to the pan.

3 Bring to the boil, then lower the heat, cover the pan, and simmer gently for about 20 minutes.

4 Strain the liquid and pour it back into the pan. Squeeze the juice from the lime and add to the pan with the fish sauce and salt and pepper to taste.

5 Bring the pan to the boil. Lower the heat, add the prawns and simmer for just 2–3 minutes.

6 Add the red chilli and spring onion. Sprinkle with coriander and serve.

COOK'S TIP

To devein the prawns, remove the shells. Cut a slit along the back of each prawn and remove the fine black vein that runs along the length of the back. Wipe clean with paper towels.

Thai Fish Soup

This is also known as Tom Yam Gung. Oriental supermarkets may sell tom yam sauce ready prepared in jars, sometimes labelled 'Chillies in Oil'.

NUTRITIONAL INFORMATION

Calories	230	Sugars	.........4g
Protein	........22g	Fat	..........12g
Carbohydrate	....9g	Saturates	.......1g

🍲 25 mins   🕐 5 mins

SERVES 4

INGREDIENTS

450 ml/16 fl oz light chicken stock

2 lime leaves, chopped

5 cm/2 inch piece lemon grass, chopped

3 tbsp lemon juice

3 tbsp Thai fish sauce

2 small, hot green chillies, deseeded and finely chopped

½ tsp sugar

8 small shiitake mushrooms, halved

450 g/1 lb raw prawns, peeled if necessary and de-veined

spring onions, to garnish

TOM YAM SAUCE

4 tbsp vegetable oil

5 garlic cloves, finely chopped

1 large shallot, finely chopped

2 large hot dried red chillies, chopped

1 tbsp dried shrimp (optional)

1 tbsp Thai fish sauce

2 tsp sugar

 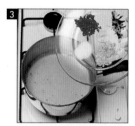 

1 First make the tom yam sauce. Heat the oil in a small pan, cook the garlic briefly until just brown, remove with a slotted spoon and set aside. Cook the shallot in the oil until brown and crisp. Remove with a slotted spoon, add the chillies, and fry until they darken. Remove and drain on paper towels. Take the pan off the hob and save the oil for later use.

2 In a small food processor or spice grinder, grind the dried shrimp, if using, then add the reserved chillies, garlic and shallot. Grind to a smooth paste. Return the paste to the original pan over a low heat. Mix in the fish sauce and sugar. Remove from the heat.

3 Heat the stock and 2 tablespoons of the tom yam sauce in a large saucepan. Add the lime leaves, lemon grass, lemon juice, fish sauce, chillies and sugar. Simmer for 2 minutes.

4 Add the mushrooms and prawns and cook a further 2–3 minutes until the prawns are cooked. Ladle into warm bowls and serve immediately, garnished with spring onion.

Thai Fish Cakes

These traditional Thai fish cakes are accompanied by a hot sweet and sour dipping sauce. Remove the chilli seeds for a milder sauce.

NUTRITIONAL INFORMATION

Calories	223	Sugars	........23g
Protein	........21g	Fat	..........4g
Carbohydrate	...25g	Saturates	.......1g

20 mins   5 mins

SERVES 4

I N G R E D I E N T S

450 g/1 lb firm white fish, skinned and roughly chopped

1 tbsp Thai fish sauce

1 tbsp red curry paste

1 kaffir lime leaf, finely shredded

2 tbsp chopped fresh coriander

1 egg

1 tsp brown sugar

large pinch salt

40 g/1½ oz green beans, thinly sliced crossways

vegetable oil, for shallow frying

S W E E T   A N D   S O U R   D I P P I N G   S A U C E

4 tbsp sugar

1 tbsp cold water

3 tbsp white rice vinegar

2 small, hot chillies, finely chopped

1 tbsp Thai fish sauce

1 For the fish cakes, put the fish, fish sauce, curry paste, coriander, lime leaf, egg, sugar and salt into a food processor. Process until smooth. Scrape into a bowl and stir in the green beans. Set aside.

2 To make the dipping sauce, put the sugar, water and rice vinegar into a small saucepan and heat gently until the sugar has dissolved. Bring to the boil and simmer for 2 minutes. Stir in the chillies and fish sauce and leave to cool.

3 Heat a frying pan with enough oil to cover the bottom generously. Divide the fish mixture into 16 little balls. Flatten into patties and fry for 1–2 minutes each side until golden. Drain on paper towels. Serve hot with the dipping sauce.

COOK'S TIP

Use any firm white fish for this recipe, such as hake, haddock, or cod. It isn't necessary to use the most expensive fish because the other flavours in the fishcakes are very strong.

Indian Potato & Pea Soup

A slightly hot and spicy Indian flavour is given to this soup by herbs and spices, including garam masala, chilli, cumin and coriander.

NUTRITIONAL INFORMATION

Calories 153	Sugars 6g
Protein 6g	Fat 6g
Carbohydrate . . .18g	Saturates 1g

 15 mins   30 mins

SERVES 4

I N G R E D I E N T S

2 tbsp vegetable oil

225 g/8 oz floury potatoes, diced

1 large onion, chopped

2 garlic cloves, crushed

1 tsp garam masala

1 tsp ground coriander

1 tsp ground cumin

1 litre/1½ pints vegetable stock

1 red chilli, chopped

100 g/3½ oz frozen peas

4 tbsp low-fat natural yogurt

salt and pepper

chopped fresh coriander,
   to garnish

COOK'S TIP

For slightly less heat, deseed the chilli before adding it to the soup. Always wash your hands well after handling chillies as they contain volatile oils that can irritate the skin and make your eyes burn if you touch your face.

1 Heat the vegetable oil in a large saucepan and add the diced potatoes, onion and garlic. Sauté gently for about 5 minutes, stirring constantly. Add the ground spices and cook for 1 minute, stirring all the time.

2 Stir in the vegetable stock and chopped red chilli and bring the mixture to the boil. Reduce the heat, cover the pan and simmer for 20 minutes.

3 Add the peas and cook for a further 5 minutes. Stir in the yogurt and season with salt and pepper to taste.

4 Pour the soup into warmed bowls, garnish with chopped coriander and serve hot with warm bread.

Vegetables with Tahini Dip

This tasty dip is great for livening up simply cooked vegetables. You can vary the vegetables according to the season.

NUTRITIONAL INFORMATION

Calories	126	Sugars	.........7g
Protein	.........11g	Fat	...........6g
Carbohydrate	....8g	Saturates	......1g

5 mins   20 mins

SERVES 4

I N G R E D I E N T S

225 g/8 oz small broccoli florets

225 g/8 oz small cauliflower florets

225 g/8 oz asparagus, sliced into 5 cm/2 inch lengths

2 small red onions, quartered

1 tbsp lime juice

2 tsp toasted sesame seeds

1 tbsp chopped fresh chives, to garnish

H O T   T A H I N I   D I P

1 tsp sunflower oil

2 garlic cloves, crushed

½–1 tsp chilli powder

2 tsp tahini

150 ml/5 fl oz low-fat natural fromage frais

2 tbsp chopped fresh chives

salt and pepper

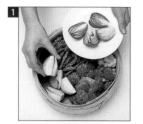  

1 Line the base of a steamer with baking paper and arrange the broccoli florets, cauliflower florets, asparagus and onion pieces on top.

2 Bring a wok or a large saucepan of water to the boil, and place the steamer on the top. Sprinkle the vegetables with lime juice for extra flavour and steam for 10 minutes until they are just tender.

3 Meanwhile, make the dip. Heat the oil in a small non-stick saucepan, add the garlic, chilli powder and seasoning to taste and fry gently for 2–3 minutes until the garlic is softened.

4 Remove the saucepan from the heat and stir in the tahini and fromage frais. Return the pan to the heat and cook gently for 1–2 minutes without boiling. Stir in the chopped chives.

5 Remove the vegetables from the steamer and place on a warmed serving platter. Sprinkle with the sesame seeds and garnish with chopped chives. Serve with the hot dip.

Thai-style Burgers

If your family likes to eat burgers, try these – they have a much more interesting flavour than conventional hamburgers.

NUTRITIONAL INFORMATION

Calories	358	Sugars	.........1g
Protein	........23g	Fat	..........29g
Carbohydrate	....2g	Saturates	.......5g

🍖 15 mins 🕐 8 mins

SERVES 4

I N G R E D I E N T S

1 small lemon grass stalk

1 small red chilli, deseeded

2 garlic cloves, peeled

2 spring onions

200 g/7 oz closed-cup mushrooms

400 g/14 oz minced pork

1 tbsp Thai fish sauce

3 tbsp chopped fresh coriander,

sunflower oil for shallow frying

2 tbsp mayonnaise

1 tbsp lime juice

salt and pepper

TO SERVE

4 sesame hamburger buns

shredded Chinese leaves

1 Place the lemon grass, chilli, garlic and spring onions in a food processor and process to a smooth paste. Add the mushrooms to the food processor and process until they are very finely chopped.

2 Add the minced pork, fish sauce and coriander. Season well with salt and pepper, then divide the mixture into 4 equal portions and shape with lightly floured hands into flat burger shapes.

3 Heat the oil in a frying pan over a medium heat. Add the burgers to the pan and fry for 6–8 minutes until cooked to your taste.

4 Meanwhile, mix the mayonnaise with the lime juice. Split the hamburger buns and spread the lime-flavoured mayonnaise on the cut surfaces. Add a few shredded Chinese leaves, top with a burger, and sandwich together. Serve immediately, while still hot.

COOK'S TIP

You can add a spoonful of your favourite relish to each burger or, alternatively, add a few pieces of crisp pickled vegetables for a change of texture.

Thai Rice Noodles

This quick and easy dish of noodles, mushrooms and tofu is very filling. If you omit the fish sauce, it can be served as a vegetarian dish.

NUTRITIONAL INFORMATION

Calories 361	Sugars 3g	
Protein 9g	Fat 12g	
Carbohydrate . . .53g	Saturates 2g	

🍲 5 mins, plus 15 mins soaking 🕐 5 mins

SERVES 4

I N G R E D I E N T S

225 g/8 oz rice stick noodles

2 tbsp vegetable oil

1 garlic clove, finely chopped

2 cm/¾ inch piece fresh ginger root, finely chopped

4 shallots, thinly sliced

70 g/2½ oz shiitake mushrooms, sliced

100 g/3½ oz firm tofu, cut into 1.5 cm/⅝ inch dice

2 tbsp light soy sauce

1 tbsp rice wine

1 tbsp Thai fish sauce

1 tbsp smooth peanut butter

1 tsp chilli sauce

2 tbsp toasted peanuts, chopped

shredded basil leaves, to serve

1 Soak the rice stick noodles in hot water for 15 minutes, or according to the package directions. Drain well.

2 Heat the oil in a frying pan or wok and stir-fry the garlic, ginger and shallots for 1–2 minutes until softened and lightly browned.

3 Add the mushrooms and stir-fry for 2–3 minutes. Stir in the tofu and toss gently to brown lightly.

4 Mix together the soy sauce, rice wine, fish sauce, peanut butter and chilli sauce, then stir into the pan.

5 Stir in the rice noodles and toss to coat evenly in the sauce. Scatter with peanuts and shredded basil leaves and serve immediately.

COOK'S TIP

For an easy storecupboard dish, replace the shiitake mushrooms with canned Chinese straw mushrooms. Alternatively, use dried shiitake mushrooms, soaked and drained before use.

Thai Crab Omelette

Do not be put off by the long list of ingredients. The omelette is served cold and so can be made entirely ahead of time.

NUTRITIONAL INFORMATION

Calories	262	Sugars	.........5g
Protein	........18g	Fat	..........19g
Carbohydrate	....5g	Saturates	.......7g

🍤 10 mins, plus 2-3 hrs chilling   🕐 10 mins

SERVES 4

INGREDIENTS

225 g/8 oz white crab meat, thawed if frozen

3 spring onions, finely chopped

1 tbsp chopped fresh coriander

1 tbsp chopped fresh chives

pinch cayenne pepper

2 tbsp vegetable oil

2 garlic cloves, crushed

1 tsp freshly grated ginger root

1 red chilli, deseeded and finely chopped

2 tbsp lime juice

2 lime leaves, shredded

2 tsp sugar

2 tsp Thai fish sauce

3 eggs, lightly beaten

4 tbsp coconut cream

1 tsp salt

spring onion slithers, to garnish

COOK'S TIP

You can also serve this omelette warm. After adding the crab, cook for 3-4 minutes to allow the mixture to heat through, then serve immediately.

1 Put the crab meat into a bowl and check for any small pieces of shell. Add the spring onions, coriander, chives and cayenne and set aside.

2 Heat half the oil in a pan, add the garlic, ginger and chilli and stir-fry for 30 seconds. Add the lime juice, lime leaves, sugar and fish sauce. Simmer for 3-4 minutes. Allow to cool, add to the crab mixture and set aside.

3 Mix the eggs, coconut cream and salt. In a frying pan, heat the remaining oil over a medium heat. Add the egg mixture and cook the omelette.

4 Spoon the crab mixture down the centre of the omelette. Fold the omelette over the filling and turn out of the pan. Cool, then refrigerate for 2-3 hours. Slice and garnish with onion slivers.

Kedgeree

Originally, kedgeree or khichri was a Hindu dish of rice and lentils, varied with fish or meat in all kinds of ways.

NUTRITIONAL INFORMATION

Calories	290	Sugars	........7g
Protein	........27g	Fat	...........11g
Carbohydrate	...23g	Saturates	.......1g

15 mins · 35 mins

SERVES 4

INGREDIENTS

450 g/1 lb undyed smoked haddock fillet

2 tbsp olive oil

1 large onion, chopped

2 garlic cloves, finely chopped

½ tsp ground turmeric

½ tsp ground cumin

1 tsp ground coriander

175 g/6 oz basmati rice

4 medium eggs

25 g/1 oz butter

1 tbsp chopped fresh parsley

TO SERVE

lemon wedges

mango chutney

1 Pour boiling water over the haddock fillet and leave for 10 minutes. Lift the fish from the cooking water, discard the skin and bones and flake the fish. Set aside. Reserve the cooking water.

2 Cook the onion in the oil in a large pan for 10 minutes over a medium heat until it begins to brown. Add the garlic and cook for 30 seconds, then add the turmeric, cumin and coriander and stir-fry for 30 seconds. When the spices smell fragrant, add the rice and stir well.

3 Measure 350 ml/12 fl oz of the haddock cooking water and add this to the pan. Stir well and bring to the boil. Cover and cook over a very low heat for 12–15 minutes until the rice is tender and the stock is absorbed.

4 Meanwhile, bring a small saucepan of water to the boil and add the eggs. When the water has returned to the boil cook the eggs for 8 minutes. Immediately drain the eggs and refresh under cold water to stop them cooking further. Shell and quarter the eggs.

5 Add the reserved fish pieces, the butter and parsley to the rice. Turn onto a large serving dish and decorate with the quartered eggs. Serve with lemon wedges and mango chutney.

Chicken Tostadas

Chicken makes a delicate yet satisfying topping for crisp tostadas, served here with a a fresh green salsa and smokey chipotle chillies.

NUTRITIONAL INFORMATION

Calories	 663	Sugars	.... 3g
Protein	.... 45g	Fat	.... 32g
Carbohydrate	... 49g	Saturates	...... 11g

15 mins   10 mins

SERVES 4–6

INGREDIENTS

6 corn tortillas

vegetable oil, for frying

450 g/1 lb skinned boned chicken breast or thigh, cut into strips or small pieces

225 ml/8 fl oz chicken stock

2 garlic cloves, finely chopped

400 g/14 oz canned refried Mexican beans

large pinch of ground cumin

225 g/8 oz grated cheese

1 tbsp chopped fresh coriander

2 ripe tomatoes, diced

handful of crisp lettuce leaves, such as cos, romaine or iceberg, shredded

4–6 radishes, diced

3 spring onions, thinly sliced

1 ripe avocado, stoned, diced or sliced and tossed with lime juice

soured cream

1–2 canned chipotle chillies in adobo marinade, or dried chipotle reconstituted, cut into thin strips

1 To make tostadas, fry the tortillas in a small amount of oil in a non-stick pan until crisp.

2 Put the chicken in a pan with the stock and garlic. Bring to the boil, then reduce the heat and cook for 1–2 minutes until the chicken begins to turn opaque.

3 Remove the pan from the heat and leave the chicken to steep in its hot liquid to cook through.

4 Heat the beans, adding a little water if necessary. Mash or blend in a food processor to form a smooth purée. Add the cumin and keep warm.

5 Reheat the tostadas under a preheated grill, if necessary. Spread the hot bean purée on the tostadas, then sprinkle with the grated cheese. Lift the cooked chicken from the liquid and divide between the tostadas. Top with the coriander, tomatoes, lettuce, radishes, spring onions, avocado, soured cream and a few strips of chipotle. Serve the tostadas immediately.

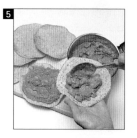

Vegetable Tostadas

Top a crisp tostada with spicy mixed vegetables, black beans and feta cheese and you have a vegetarian feast.

NUTRITIONAL INFORMATION

Calories	.541	Sugars	.10g
Protein	.25g	Fat	.20g
Carbohydrate	.69g	Saturates	.9g

 15 mins   20 mins

SERVES 4

INGREDIENTS

4 corn tortillas

vegetable oil, for frying

2–3 tbsp extra-virgin olive oil or vegetable oil

2 potatoes, diced

1 carrot, diced

3 garlic cloves, finely chopped

1 red pepper, deseeded and diced

1 tsp mild chilli powder

1 tsp paprika

½ tsp ground cumin

3–4 ripe tomatoes, diced

115 g/4 oz green beans, blanched and cut into bite-sized lengths

several large pinches dried oregano

400 g/14 oz cooked black beans

225 g/8 oz crumbled feta cheese

3–4 leaves cos lettuce, shredded

3–4 spring onions, thinly sliced

1 To make tostadas, fry the tortillas in a small amount of oil in a non-stick pan until crisp.

2 Heat the olive oil in a frying pan, add the potatoes and carrot and cook until softened. Add the garlic, red pepper, chilli powder, paprika and cumin. Cook for 2–3 minutes until the pepper has softened.

3 Add the tomatoes, green beans and oregano. Cook for 8–10 minutes until the vegetables are tender and form a sauce-like mixture. The mixture should not be too dry; add a little water if necessary, to keep it moist.

4 Heat the black beans in a saucepan with a tiny amount of water, and keep them warm. Reheat the tostadas under a preheated grill.

5 Layer the beans over the hot tostadas, then sprinkle with the cheese and top with a few spoonfuls of the hot vegetables in sauce. Serve at once, each tostada sprinkled with the lettuce and spring onions.

Fragrant Black Bean Chilli

Enjoy this chillied bean stew Mexican style with soft tortillas, or Californian style in a bowl with crisp tortillas chips crumbled in.

NUTRITIONAL INFORMATION

Calories	428	Sugars	.......11g
Protein	........31g	Fat	..........10g
Carbohydrate	...53g	Saturates	.......2g

20 mins   2½ hrs

SERVES 4

INGREDIENTS

400 g/14 oz dried black beans, soaked overnight and drained

2 tbsp olive oil

1 onion, chopped

5 garlic cloves, coarsely chopped

2 rashers bacon, diced (optional)

½–1 tsp ground cumin

½–1 tsp mild red chilli powder

1 red pepper, diced

1 carrot, diced

400 g/14 oz fresh tomatoes, diced, or chopped canned tomatoes

1 bunch fresh coriander, coarsely chopped

salt and pepper

1 Put the beans in a pan, cover with water and bring to the boil. Boil for 10 minutes, then reduce the heat and simmer for about 1½ hours until tender. Drain well when cooked, reserving 225 ml/8 fl oz of the cooking liquid.

COOK'S TIP

You can use canned beans, if wished: drain off the liquid from the can and use 225 ml/ 8 fl oz water for the liquid added in Step 4.

2 Heat the oil in a frying pan. Add the onion and garlic and fry for 2 minutes, stirring. Stir in the bacon, if using, and cook, stirring occasionally, until the bacon is cooked and the onion is soft.

3 Stir in the cumin and chilli powder and cook briefly. Add the red pepper, carrot and tomatoes. Cook over a medium heat for about 5 minutes.

4 Add half the coriander and the beans and their reserved liquid. Season with salt and pepper. Simmer for 30–45 minutes or until thickened.

5 Stir through the remaining coriander, adjust the seasoning and serve.

 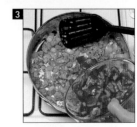 

Migas

A wonderful brunch or late-night supper dish, this is made by scrambling egg with chillies, tomatoes and crisp tortilla chips.

NUTRITIONAL INFORMATION

Calories	441	Sugars	. . . . .5g
Protein	. . . . . . .22g	Fat	. . . . .20g
Carbohydrate	. . .46g	Saturates	. . . . . . .8g

 10 mins 10 mins

SERVES 4

I N G R E D I E N T S

2 tbsp butter

6 garlic cloves, finely chopped

1 fresh green chilli, such as jalapeño or serrano, deseeded and diced

1½ tsp ground cumin

6 ripe tomatoes, coarsely chopped

8 eggs, lightly beaten

8–10 corn tortillas, cut into strips and fried until crisp, or an equal amount of not too salty tortilla chips

4 tbsp chopped fresh coriander

3–4 spring onions, thinly sliced

mild chilli powder, to garnish

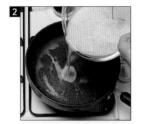

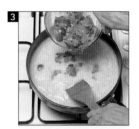

1 Melt half the butter in a pan. Add the garlic and chilli and cook until softened, but not browned. Add the cumin and cook for 30 seconds, stirring, then add the tomatoes and cook over a medium heat for a further 3–4 minutes, or until the tomato juices have evaporated. Remove from the pan and set aside.

2 Melt the remaining butter in a frying pan over a low heat and pour in the beaten eggs. Cook, stirring, until the egg begins to set.

3 Add the chilli tomato mixture, stirring gently to mix into the eggs.

4 Carefully add the tortilla strips or chips and continue cooking, stirring once or twice, until the eggs are the consistency you wish. The tortillas should be pliable and chewy.

5 Transfer to a serving plate and surround with the fresh coriander and spring onions. Garnish with a little sprinkling of mild chilli powder and serve the dish immediately.

COOK'S TIP
Serve the migas with soured cream or crème fraîche on top, to melt seductively into the spicy eggs.

Potato-filled Naan Breads

This is a filling Indian sandwich. Spicy potatoes fill the naan breads, which are served with a cool cucumber raita and lime pickle.

NUTRITIONAL INFORMATION

Calories	244	Sugars	.........7g
Protein	.........8g	Fat	...........8g
Carbohydrate	...37g	Saturates	......1g

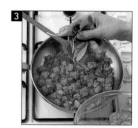

10 mins   25 mins

SERVES 4

INGREDIENTS

225 g/8 oz waxy potatoes, scrubbed and diced

1 tbsp vegetable oil

1 onion, chopped

2 garlic cloves, crushed

1 tsp ground cumin

1 tsp ground coriander

½ tsp chilli powder

1 tbsp tomato purée

3 tbsp vegetable stock

75 g/2¾ oz baby spinach, shredded

4 small or 2 large naan breads

lime pickle, to serve

RAITA

150 ml/5 fl oz low-fat natural yogurt

4 tbsp diced cucumber

1 tbsp chopped mint

1 Cook the diced potatoes in a saucepan of boiling water for 10 minutes. Drain thoroughly.

2 Heat the vegetable oil in a separate saucepan and cook the onion and garlic for 3 minutes, stirring. Add the spices and cook for a further 2 minutes.

3 Stir in the potatoes, tomato purée, vegetable stock and shredded spinach. Cook for a further 5 minutes or until the potatoes are tender.

4 Warm the naan breads in a preheated oven, 150°C/300°F/Gas Mark 2, for about 2 minutes.

5 To make the raita, mix the yogurt, cucumber and mint together in a small bowl.

6 Remove the naan breads from the oven. Using a sharp knife, cut a pocket in the side of each naan bread. Spoon the spicy potato mixture into each pocket.

7 Serve the filled naan breads at once, accompanied by the raita and lime pickle.

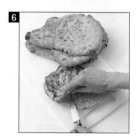

COOK'S TIP

To give the raita a much stronger flavour, make it in advance and leave to chill in the refrigerator until you are ready to serve the meal.

Chicken Jalfrezi

This is a quick and tasty way to use leftover roast chicken. The sauce can also be used for any cooked poultry, lamb or beef.

NUTRITIONAL INFORMATION

Calories	270	Sugars	. . . . .3g
Protein	. . . . .36g	Fat	. . . . .11g
Carbohydrate	. . . .7g	Saturates	. . . . . .2g

25 mins   15 mins

SERVES 4

INGREDIENTS

1 tsp mustard oil

3 tbsp vegetable oil

1 large onion, chopped finely

3 garlic cloves, crushed

1 tbsp tomato purée

2 tomatoes, skinned and chopped

1 tsp ground turmeric

½ tsp cumin seeds, ground

½ tsp coriander seeds, ground

½ tsp chilli powder

½ tsp garam masala

1 tsp red wine vinegar

1 small red pepper, chopped

125 g/4½ oz frozen broad
   beans

500 g/1 lb 2 oz cooked chicken, cut into
   bite-sized pieces

salt

sprigs of fresh coriander,
   to garnish

1 Heat the mustard oil in a large frying pan set over a high heat for about 1 minute until it begins to smoke.

2 Add the vegetable oil, reduce the heat and then add the onion and the garlic. Fry the garlic and onion until they are golden and softened.

3 Add the tomato purée, chopped tomatoes, turmeric, ground cumin and coriander seeds, chilli powder, garam masala and wine vinegar to the frying pan. Stir the mixture until fragrant.

4 Add the red pepper and broad beans and stir for 2 minutes until the pepper is softened. Stir in the chicken, and salt to taste.

5 Simmer gently for 6–8 minutes until the chicken is heated through and the beans are tender.

6 Serve immediately garnished with sprigs of coriander and accompanied by basmati rice.

Mixed Vegetable Balti

Any combination of vegetables or pulses can be used in this recipe.
It would make a good dish to serve to vegetarians.

NUTRITIONAL INFORMATION

Calories 207	Sugars 6g
Protein 8g	Fat 9g
Carbohydrate . . .24g	Saturates 1g

10 mins   1 hour 10 mins

SERVES 4

I N G R E D I E N T S

225 g/8 oz split yellow peas, washed

3 tbsp oil

1 tsp onion seeds

2 onions, sliced

125 g/4½ oz courgettes, sliced

125 g/4½ oz potatoes, cut into
    1 cm/½ inch cubes

125 g/4½ oz carrots, sliced

1 small aubergine, sliced

225 g/8 oz tomatoes, chopped

300 ml/½ pint water

3 garlic cloves, chopped

1 tsp ground cumin

1 tsp ground coriander

1 tsp salt

2 fresh green chillies, sliced

½ tsp garam masala

2 tbsp chopped fresh coriander

1 Put the split peas into a saucepan and cover with salted water. Bring to the boil and simmer for 30 minutes. Drain the peas and keep warm.

2 Heat the oil in a balti pan or wok, add the onion seeds and fry, stirring, until they start to pop.

3 Add the sliced onions and stir-fry until they are soft and golden brown.

4 Add the prepared courgettes, potatoes, carrots and aubergine to the pan and stir-fry for 2 minutes.

5 Stir in the chopped tomatoes, water, garlic, cumin, ground coriander, salt, sliced chillies, garam masala and the reserved split peas.

6 Bring to the boil, then simmer for 15 minutes until all the vegetables are tender, stirring from time to time.

7 Stir the chopped fresh coriander into the spiced vegetables and serve.

Meatballs in Spicy Sauce

These meatballs, flecked with fresh coriander, are delicious served with warm crusty bread to mop up the spicy tomato sauce.

NUTRITIONAL INFORMATION

Calories 95   Sugars 2.7g
Protein . . . . .4.5g   Fat 5.8g
Carbohydrate . . .6.6g   Saturates 2.3g

  20 mins   1 hr 10 mins

SERVES 4

I N G R E D I E N T S

225 g/8 oz floury potatoes, diced

225 g/8 oz minced beef or lamb

1 onion, finely chopped

1 tbsp chopped fresh coriander

1 celery stick, finely chopped

2 garlic cloves, crushed

2 tbsp butter

1 tbsp vegetable oil

salt and pepper

chopped fresh coriander, to garnish

S A U C E

1 tbsp vegetable oil

1 onion, finely chopped

150 ml/5 fl oz cold vegetable stock

2 tsp soft brown sugar

400 g/14 oz canned chopped tomatoes

1 green chilli, chopped

1 tsp paprika

2 tsp cornflour

1 Cook the diced potatoes in boiling water for 10 minutes until cooked through. Drain well and transfer to a large mixing bowl. Mash until smooth.

2 Add the minced beef or lamb, onion, coriander, celery and garlic and mix together well.

3 Bring the mixture together with your hands to form a ball. Divide it up and roll it into 20 small balls.

4 To make the sauce, heat the oil in a pan and sauté the onion for 5 minutes. Put the cornflour in a small bowl and very gradually stir in the stock. Add to the pan with the remaining sauce ingredients and bring to the boil, stirring constantly. Simmer for 20 minutes.

5 Meanwhile, heat the butter and oil for the meatballs in a frying pan. Add the balls in batches and cook for 10–15 minutes until browned, turning frequently. Keep warm whilst cooking the remainder. Serve the meatballs in a warm, shallow ovenproof dish with the sauce poured around them and garnished with the fresh coriander.

Stir-fried Beef & Noodles

A quick-and-easy stir-fry for any day of the week, this is a good one-pan main dish. Serve a simple green side salad to complete the meal.

NUTRITIONAL INFORMATION

Calories	566	Sugars	.........9g
Protein	........39g	Fat	..........22g
Carbohydrate	...55g	Saturates	.......7g

 10 mins   ⏱ 15 mins

SERVES 4

I N G R E D I E N T S

1 bunch spring onions

2 tbsp sunflower oil

1 garlic clove, crushed

1 tsp fresh root ginger, finely chopped

500 g/1 lb 2 oz tender beef, cut into thin strips

1 large red pepper, deseeded and sliced

1 small red chilli, deseeded and chopped

350 g/12 oz fresh beansprouts

1 small lemon grass stalk, finely chopped

25 g/1 oz smooth peanut butter

4 tbsp coconut milk

1 tbsp rice vinegar

1 tbsp soy sauce

1 tsp soft light brown sugar

250 g/9 oz medium egg noodles

salt and pepper

1 Trim and thinly slice the spring onions, setting aside some slices to use as a garnish.

2 Heat the oil in a frying pan or wok over a high heat. Add the spring onions, garlic and ginger and then stir-fry for 2–3 minutes to soften. Add the beef and continue stir-frying for 4–5 minutes until browned evenly.

3 Add the red pepper and stir-fry for a further 3–4 minutes. Add the chilli and beansprouts and stir-fry for 2 minutes. Mix together the lemon grass, peanut butter, coconut milk, vinegar, soy sauce and sugar, then stir this mixture into the wok.

4 Meanwhile, cook the egg noodles in boiling lightly salted water for 4 minutes, or according to the packet directions. Drain and stir into the frying pan or wok, tossing to mix evenly with the beef mixture.

5 Season with salt and pepper to taste. Sprinkle with the reserved spring onions and serve while still hot.

Red-hot Beef with Cashews

Hot and spicy, these quick-cooked beef strips are very tempting. Serve them with lots of plain rice and cucumber slices to offset the heat.

NUTRITIONAL INFORMATION

Calories . . . . .257 Sugars 1g
Protein . . . . .32g Fat 13g
Carbohydrate . . . .3g Saturates 4g

15 mins, plus 2–3 hrs marinating   8 mins

SERVES 4

I N G R E D I E N T S

500 g/1 lb 2 oz boneless, lean beef sirloin, thinly sliced

1 tsp vegetable oil

M A R I N A D E

1 tbsp sesame seeds

1 garlic clove, chopped

1 tbsp fresh root ginger, finely chopped

1 red bird-eye chilli, chopped

2 tbsp dark soy sauce

1 tsp red curry paste

T O F I N I S H

1 tsp sesame oil

4 tbsp unsalted cashew nuts

1 spring onion, thickly sliced diagonally

cucumber slices, to garnish

1 Cut the beef into 1 cm/½ inch wide strips. Place them in a large, non-metallic bowl.

2 To make the marinade, toast the sesame seeds in a heavy-based pan over a medium heat for 2–3 minutes until golden brown, shaking the pan occasionally.

3 Place the seeds in a pestle and mortar with the garlic, ginger and chilli, and grind to a smooth paste. Add the soy sauce and curry paste and mix well.

4 Spoon the paste over the beef strips and toss well to coat the meat evenly. Cover and leave to marinate in the refrigerator for 2–3 hours, or overnight.

5 Heat a heavy frying pan or griddle until very hot and brush with vegetable oil. Add the beef strips and cook quickly, turning often, until lightly browned. Remove from the heat and spoon onto a hot serving dish.

6 Heat the sesame oil in a small pan and quickly fry the cashew nuts until golden. Take care that they do not burn. Add the spring onions and stir-fry for 30 seconds. Sprinkle the mixture on top of the beef strips and serve immediately garnished with cucumber slices.

Hot Beef & Coconut Curry

The heat of the chillies in this curry is balanced and softened by the coconut milk, producing a creamy-textured, rich and lavishly spiced dish.

NUTRITIONAL INFORMATION

Calories 230	Sugars 6g	
Protein 29g	Fat 10g	
Carbohydrate 8g	Saturates 3g	

🌶 🌶

🥘 15 mins   🕐 40 mins

SERVES 4

INGREDIENTS

400 ml/14 fl oz coconut milk

2 tbsp Thai red curry paste

2 garlic cloves, crushed

500 g/1lb 2 oz braising steak

2 kaffir lime leaves, shredded

3 tbsp kaffir lime juice

2 tbsp Thai fish sauce

1 large red chilli, deseeded and sliced

½ tsp turmeric

½ tsp salt

2 tbsp fresh basil leaves, chopped

2 tbsp fresh coriander leaves, chopped

shredded coconut, to garnish

boiled rice, to serve

1 Place the coconut milk in a large pan. Bring to the boil and simmer gently for about 10 minutes until thickened. Stir in the red curry paste and garlic and simmer for a further 5 minutes.

2 Cut the braising steak into chunks about 2 cm/¾ inch square and add them to the pan. Bring to the boil, stirring, then lower the heat.

3 Add the lime leaves, lime juice, fish sauce, chilli, turmeric and salt. Cover the pan and simmer for 20–25 minutes until the meat is tender, adding a little water if the sauce looks too dry.

4 Stir in the basil and coriander and adjust the seasoning to taste. Sprinkle with coconut and serve immediately with plain boiled rice.

COOK'S TIP

This recipe uses one of the larger, milder red chilli peppers – either fresno or Dutch – simply because they give more colour to the dish. If you prefer to use small Thai, or bird-eye, chillies, you'll still need only one as they are much hotter.

Red Lamb Curry

This curry uses the typically red-hot chilli flavour of Thai red curry paste, made with dried red chillies, to give it a warm, russet-red colour.

NUTRITIONAL INFORMATION

Calories	363	Sugars	........11g
Protein	........29g	Fat	..........19g
Carbohydrate	...21g	Saturates	.......6g

15 mins   35–40 mins

SERVES 4

INGREDIENTS

500 g/1 lb 2 oz boneless lean leg of lamb

2 tbsp vegetable oil

1 large onion, sliced

2 garlic cloves, crushed

2 tbsp red curry paste

150 ml/5 fl oz coconut milk

1 tbsp soft light brown sugar

1 large red pepper, seeded and thickly sliced

120 ml/4 fl oz lamb or beef stock

1 tbsp fish sauce

2 tbsp lime juice

227 g/8 oz can water chestnuts, drained

2 tbsp fresh coriander, chopped

2 tbsp fresh basil, chopped

salt and pepper

boiled jasmine rice, to serve

fresh basil leaves, to garnish

1 Trim the meat and cut it into 3 cm/1¼ inch cubes. Heat the oil in a large frying pan or wok over a high heat and stir-fry the onion and garlic for 2–3 minutes to soften. Add the meat and continue to stir-fry the mixture quickly over a high heat until the meat is lightly browned.

2 Stir in the curry paste and cook for a few seconds, then add the coconut milk and sugar and bring to the boil. Reduce the heat and simmer for 15 minutes, stirring occasionally.

3 Stir in the red pepper, stock, fish sauce and lime juice. Cover the pan and continue simmering for a further 15 minutes, or until the meat is tender.

4 Add the water chestnuts, coriander and basil, adjust the seasoning to taste. Serve with jasmine rice garnished with fresh basil leaves.

Chicken & Mango Stir-Fry

A colourful, exotic mix of flavours that works surprisingly well, this dish is easy and quick to cook – ideal for a mid-week family meal.

NUTRITIONAL INFORMATION

Calories 200	Sugars 5g
Protein 23g	Fat 6g
Carbohydrate 7g	Saturates 1g

🍴 15 mins   🕐 15 mins

SERVES 4

INGREDIENTS

6 boneless, skinless chicken thighs

2 tsp grated fresh root ginger

1 garlic clove, crushed

1 small red chilli, seeded

1 large red pepper

4 spring onions

200 g/7 oz mangetouts

100 g/3½ oz baby corn cobs

1 large, firm, ripe mango

2 tbsp sunflower oil

1 tbsp light soy sauce

3 tbsp rice wine or sherry

1 tsp sesame oil

salt and pepper

snipped chives, to garnish

1 Cut the chicken into long, thin strips and place in a bowl. Mix together the ginger, garlic and chilli, then stir into the chicken strips to coat them evenly.

2 Slice the pepper thinly, cutting diagonally. Trim and diagonally slice the spring onions. Cut the mangetouts and corn in half diagonally. Peel the mango, remove the stone and slice thinly.

3 Heat the oil in a large frying pan or wok over a high heat. Add the chicken and stir-fry for 4–5 minutes until just turning golden brown. Add the peppers and stir-fry over a medium heat for 4–5 minutes to soften them.

4 Add the spring onions, mangetouts and corn and stir-fry for a further minute.

5 Mix together the soy sauce, rice wine or sherry and sesame oil and stir the mixture into the wok. Add the mango and stir gently for 1 minute to heat thoroughly.

6 Adjust the seasoning with salt and pepper to taste and serve immediately, garnished with chives.

Spiced Coriander Chicken

These simple Thai marinated chicken breasts are packed with the powerful flavours of chilli, ginger, coriander, lime and coconut.

NUTRITIONAL INFORMATION

Calories 171   Sugars 8g

Protein . . . . .31g   Fat 2g

Carbohydrate . . . .9g   Saturates 0.5g

1 hr 15 mins, plus 1 hr marinating   🕐 15 mins

SERVES 4

INGREDIENTS

4 boneless, skinless chicken breasts

2 garlic cloves, peeled

1 fresh green chilli, deseeded

2 cm/¾ inch piece fresh ginger root, peeled

4 tbsp chopped, fresh coriander

rind of 1 lime, finely grated

3 tbsp lime juice

2 tbsp light soy sauce

1 tbsp caster sugar

175 ml/6 fl oz coconut milk

plain boiled rice, to serve

cucumber and radish slices, to garnish

1 Using a sharp knife, cut 3 deep slashes into the skinned side of each chicken breast. Place the breasts in a single layer in a wide, non-metallic dish.

2 Put the garlic, chilli, ginger, coriander, lime rind and juice, soy sauce, caster sugar and coconut milk in a food processor and process to a smooth purée.

3 Spread the purée over both sides of the chicken breasts, coating them evenly. Cover the dish and leave to marinate in the refrigerator for about 1 hour.

4 Lift the chicken from the marinade, drain off the excess and place in a grill pan. Grill under a preheated grill for 12–15 minutes until thoroughly and evenly cooked.

5 Meanwhile, place the remaining marinade in a saucepan and bring to the boil. Lower the heat and simmer for several minutes to heat thoroughly. Serve with the chicken breasts, accompanied with rice and garnished with cucumber and radish slices.

Green Chicken Curry

Thai curries are traditionally very hot. Serve with plenty of plain boiled rice to absorb the thin, highly spiced juices.

NUTRITIONAL INFORMATION

Calories 193	Sugars 9g
Protein 22g	Fat 8g
Carbohydrate 9g	Saturates 1g

  15 mins   40 mins

SERVES 4

INGREDIENTS

6 boneless, skinless chicken thighs

400 ml/14 fl oz coconut milk

2 garlic cloves, crushed

2 tbsp Thai fish sauce

2 tbsp Thai green curry paste

12 baby aubergines, also called Thai pea aubergines

3 green chillies, finely chopped

3 kaffir lime leaves, shredded

4 tbsp fresh coriander, chopped

boiled rice, to serve

1 Cut the chicken meat into bite-sized pieces. Pour the coconut milk into a large pan or wok. Set it over a high heat and bring to the boil.

COOK'S TIP

Small baby aubergines, or 'pea aubergines' as they are called in Thailand, are traditionally used in this curry, but they are not always easily available outside the country. You may be able to find them in an Oriental food shop, but if not you can use chopped ordinary aubergine as a substitute.

2 Add the chicken, garlic and fish sauce to the pan and bring back to the boil. Lower the heat and simmer gently for 30 minutes, or until the chicken is just tender. Stir the pan occasionally.

3 When the chicken is tender remove it from the mixture using a perforated spoon. Place the cooked chicken in a warmed dish and set it aside to keep warm while you prepare the paste.

4 Stir the green curry paste into the pan, add the aubergines, chillies and lime leaves and simmer for 5 minutes.

5 Return the chicken to the pan and bring to the boil. Adjust the seasoning to taste with salt and pepper, stir in the coriander and serve with boiled rice.

Crispy Duck with Noodles

A robustly flavoured dish that makes a substantial main course. Serve it with a refreshing cucumber salad or a light vegetable stir-fry.

NUTRITIONAL INFORMATION

Calories	433	Sugars	.........7g
Protein	........25g	Fat	..........10g
Carbohydrate	...59g	Saturates	.......2g

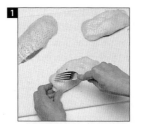

20 mins, plus 1hr marinating

30 mins

SERVES 4

INGREDIENTS

3 duck breasts, total weight about 400 g/14 oz

2 garlic cloves, crushed

1½ tsp chilli paste

1 tbsp honey

3 tbsp dark soy sauce

½ tsp five-spice powder

250 g/9 oz rice stick noodles

1 tsp vegetable oil

1 tsp sesame oil

2 spring onion, sliced

100 g/3½ oz mangetouts

2 tbsp tamarind juice

sesame seeds, to garnish

1 Prick the duck breast skin all over with a fork and place in a deep dish.

2 Mix together the garlic, chilli, honey, soy sauce and five-spice powder, then pour over the duck. Turn the breasts to coat evenly, then cover and marinate in the refrigerator for at least 1 hour.

3 Meanwhile, soak the rice noodles in hot water for 15 minutes. Drain well.

4 Drain the duck breasts from the marinade. Reserve the marinade and grill the duck on a rack under high heat for about 10 minutes, turning them over occasionally, until they become a rich golden brown. Transfer the duck breasts to a plate, slice them thinly and keep warm.

5 Heat the vegetable and sesame oils in a pan and toss the spring onions and mangetouts for 2 minutes. Stir in the reserved marinade and tamarind and bring quickly to the boil.

6 Add the sliced duck and noodles to the pan and toss to heat thoroughly. Serve immediately, sprinkled with sesame seeds to garnish.

Chicken with Vinegar

Roasted garlic and mixed spices give an evocative flavour to this tangy chicken dish, a speciality of Valladolid in the Yucatan peninsula.

NUTRITIONAL INFORMATION

Calories 313	Sugars 6g
Protein 15g	Fat 22g
Carbohydrate . . .14g	Saturates 3g

20 mins, plus 1 hr marinating   25 mins

SERVES 4

I N G R E D I E N T S

8 small boned chicken thighs

chicken stock

15–20 garlic cloves, unpeeled

1 tsp coarsely ground black pepper

½ tsp ground cloves

2 tsp crumbled dried oregano or ½ tsp crushed or powdered bay leaves

about ½ tsp salt

1 tbsp lime juice

1 tsp cumin seeds, lightly toasted

1 tbsp flour, plus extra for dredging the chicken

3–4 onions, thinly sliced

2 fresh chillies, preferably mildish yellow ones, such as Mexican Guero or similar Turkish or Greek chillies, deseeded and sliced

vegetable oil, for frying

100 ml/3½ fl oz cider or sherry vinegar

1 Place the chicken in a pan with enough stock to cover. Bring to the boil, then reduce the heat and simmer for 5 minutes. Remove from the heat and allow the chicken to cool and continue to cook in the stock.

2 Meanwhile, roast the garlic cloves in a dry frying pan until they are lightly browned on all sides and tender inside. Cool, then squeeze the flesh from the skins and place in a bowl.

3 Grind the garlic, pepper, cloves, oregano, salt, lime juice and ³/₄ teaspoon of the cumin seeds. Add the flour.

4 When the chicken is cool, remove from the stock and pat dry. Reserve the stock. Rub the chicken with about two-thirds of the garlic-spice paste and marinate for 1-12 hours in the refrigerator.

5 Fry the onions and chillies in a little oil until golden brown. Pour in the vinegar and remaining cumin seeds, cook for a few minutes, then add the reserved stock and remaining spice paste. Boil, stirring, for 10 minutes.

6 Dredge the chicken in flour. Fry in oil until the chicken until lightly browned, then remove from the pan. Serve with the onion mixture.

Ginger Beef with Chilli

Serve these fruity, hot and spicy steaks with noodles. Use a non-stick ridged frying pan to cook with a minimum of fat.

NUTRITIONAL INFORMATION

Calories ....179 Sugars 8g
Protein ....21g Fat 6g
Carbohydrate ....8g Saturates 2g

15 mins, plus
30 mins chilling   10 mins

SERVES 4

I N G R E D I E N T S

4 lean beef steaks (such as rump, sirloin or fillet), 100 g/3½ oz each

2 tbsp ginger wine

2.5 cm/1 inch piece fresh root ginger, finely chopped

1 garlic clove, crushed

1 tsp ground chilli

1 tsp vegetable oil

salt and pepper

red chilli strips, to garnish

TO SERVE

freshly cooked noodles

2 spring onions, shredded

RELISH

225 g/8 oz fresh pineapple

1 small red pepper

1 red chilli

2 tbsp light soy sauce

1 piece stem ginger in syrup, drained and chopped

1 Trim any excess fat from the beef if necessary. Using a meat mallet or covered rolling pin, pound the steaks until 1 cm/½ inch thick. Season on both sides and place in a shallow dish.

2 Mix the ginger wine, finely chopped ginger root, garlic and chilli and pour the mixture over the meat. Cover and chill for 30 minutes.

3 Meanwhile, make the relish. Peel and finely chop the pineapple and place it in a bowl. Halve, deseed and finely chop the pepper and chilli. Stir into the pineapple, together with the soy sauce and stem ginger. Cover and chill until required.

4 Brush a grill pan with the oil and heat until very hot. Drain the steaks and add to the pan, pressing down to seal. Lower the heat and cook for 5 minutes. Turn the steaks over and cook for a further 5 minutes.

5 Drain the steaks on kitchen paper and transfer to serving plates. Garnish with chilli strips, and serve with noodles, spring onions and the relish.

Chicken with a Yogurt Crust

A spicy, Indian-style coating is baked around lean chicken to give a full flavour. Serve with a tomato, cucumber and coriander relish.

NUTRITIONAL INFORMATION

Calories ....176 Sugars 5g
Protein ....30g Fat 4g
Carbohydrate ....5g Saturates 1g

10 mins   35 mins

SERVES 4

INGREDIENTS

1 garlic clove, crushed

2.5 cm/1 inch piece fresh root ginger, finely chopped

1 fresh green chilli, deseeded and finely chopped

6 tbsp low-fat natural yogurt

1 tbsp tomato purée

1 tsp ground turmeric

1 tsp garam masala

1 tbsp lime juice

4 boneless, skinless chicken breasts, each 125 g/4½ oz

salt and pepper

wedges of lime or lemon, to serve

RELISH

4 medium tomatoes

¼ cucumber

1 small red onion

2 tbsp chopped fresh coriander

1 Preheat the oven to 190°C/375°F/Gas Mark 5. Place the garlic, ginger, chilli, yogurt, tomato purée, spices, lime juice and seasoning in a bowl and mix to combine all the ingredients.

2 Wash the chicken breasts and pat them dry, using absorbent kitchen paper. Place the pieces on a baking sheet or in a low-sided ovenproof dish.

3 Brush or spread the spicy yogurt mix over the chicken and bake in the oven for 30–35 minutes until the meat is tender and cooked through.

4 Meanwhile, make the relish. Finely chop the tomatoes, cucumber and red onion and mix together with the chopped coriander. Season with salt and pepper to taste, cover and chill in the refrigerator until required.

5 Serve hot with the relish and lemon or lime wedges. Alternatively, allow to cool, chill for at least 1 hour and serve sliced as part of a salad.

Barbecued Indian Chicken

An Indian-influenced barbecue dish that is delicious served with warm naan bread and a fresh cucumber raita.

NUTRITIONAL INFORMATION

Calories 228	Sugars 12g	
Protein 28g	Fat 8g	
Carbohydrate ...12g	Saturates 2g	

20 mins   10 mins

SERVES 4

INGREDIENTS

4 boneless, skinless chicken breasts

2 tbsp curry paste

1 tbsp sunflower oil

1 tbsp light muscovado sugar

1 tsp ground ginger

½ tsp ground cumin

TO SERVE

warm naan bread

green salad leaves

CUCUMBER RAITA

¼ cucumber

salt

150 ml/5 fl oz low-fat natural yogurt

¼ tsp chilli powder

1 Place the chicken breasts between 2 sheets of baking paper. Flatten them with a meat mallet or a rolling pin.

2 Mix the curry paste, oil, sugar, ginger and cumin. Spread the mixture over both sides of the chicken.

3 To make the raita, peel the cucumber and scoop out the seeds with a spoon.

Grate the flesh, sprinkle with salt, place in a sieve and let stand for 10 minutes. Rinse off the salt and squeeze out any moisture. Mix with the yogurt and the chilli powder. Leave to chill until required.

4 Transfer the chicken to an oiled rack and barbecue over hot coals for 10 minutes, turning once. Serve with naan bread, raita and salad leaves.

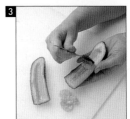

Cajun Chicken Gumbo

This complete main course is cooked in one saucepan. If you are cooking for one, halve the ingredients – the cooking time should stay the same.

NUTRITIONAL INFORMATION

Calories 425	Sugars 8g
Protein 34g	Fat 12g
Carbohydrate ...48g	Saturates 3g

 5 mins 25 mins

SERVES 2

INGREDIENTS

1 tbsp sunflower oil

4 chicken thighs

1 small onion, diced

2 sticks celery, diced

1 small green pepper, diced

90 g/3 oz long grain rice

300 ml/10 fl oz chicken stock

1 small red chilli

225 g/8 oz okra

15 ml/1 tbsp tomato purée

salt and pepper

1 Heat the oil in a wide pan and fry the chicken until golden. Remove the chicken from the pan.

2 Stir in the diced onion, celery and pepper and fry them for 1 minute. Pour off any excess oil.

3 Add the rice and fry, stirring, for a further minute. Add the stock and heat until boiling. Thinly slice the chilli and trim the okra. Add to the pan with the tomato purée. Season to taste.

4 Return the chicken to the pan and stir. Cover tightly and simmer gently for 15 minutes, or until the rice is tender, the chicken is thoroughly cooked and the liquid absorbed. Stir occasionally and if it becomes too dry, add a little extra stock.

COOK'S TIP

The whole chilli makes the dish hot and spicy – if you prefer a milder flavour, discard the seeds of the chilli carefully before you slice it.

Chicken Tikka

For this very popular dish, small pieces of chicken are marinated for a minimum of 3 hours in yogurt and spices.

NUTRITIONAL INFORMATION

Calories	327	Sugars	.........2g
Protein	........61g	Fat	...........8g
Carbohydrate	....3g	Saturates	.......1g

15 mins, plus 3 hrs marinating   10 mins

SERVES 6

I N G R E D I E N T S

1 tsp finely chopped fresh root ginger

1 tsp fresh garlic, crushed

½ tsp ground coriander

½ tsp ground cumin

1 tsp chilli powder

3 tbsp yogurt

1 tsp salt

2 tbsp lemon juice

a few drops of red food colouring

1 tbsp tomato purée

1.5 kg/3 lb 5 oz chicken breast

1 onion, sliced

3 tbsp oil

TO GARNISH

6 green salad leaves

1 lemon, cut into wedges

1 Blend the ginger, garlic, ground coriander, ground cumin and chilli powder in a large mixing bowl.

2 Add the yogurt, salt, lemon juice, red food colouring and tomato purée.

3 Cut the chicken into bite-sized pieces. Add it to the spice mixture and toss to coat well. Leave to marinate for at least 3 hours, preferably overnight.

4 Arrange the onion in the bottom of a heatproof dish. Carefully drizzle half of the oil over the onions.

5 Arrange the marinated chicken pieces on top of the onions and cook under a pre-heated grill, turning once and basting with the remaining oil, for about 10 minutes, until the chicken is cooked right through and tender.

6 Serve the chicken tikka on a bed of green salad leaves, accompanied by warm naan bread and garnished with the lemon wedges to squeeze.

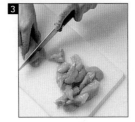

Baked Fish with Basil

Almost any whole fish can be cooked by this method, but snapper, sea bass and John Dory are particularly good with the Thai flavours.

NUTRITIONAL INFORMATION

Calories .... .267 Sugars 9g
Protein ....38g Fat 8g
Carbohydrate ....11g Saturates 2g

15 mins   30 mins

SERVES 4

INGREDIENTS

handful of fresh sweet basil leaves

750 g/1 lb 10 oz whole red snapper, sea bass or John Dory, cleaned

2 tbsp groundnut oil

2 tbsp Thai fish sauce

2 garlic cloves, crushed

1 tsp galangal or ginger root, finely grated

2 large fresh red chillies, sliced diagonally

1 yellow pepper, deseeded and diced

1 tbsp palm sugar

1 tbsp rice vinegar

2 tbsp water or fish stock

2 tomatoes, deseeded and sliced into thin wedges

1 Reserve a few fresh basil leaves for garnish and tuck the rest inside the body cavity of the fish.

2 Heat 1 tablespoon of oil in a wide frying pan and fry the fish quickly to brown, turning once. Place the fish on a large piece of foil in a roasting tin and spoon over the fish sauce. Wrap the foil over the fish loosely and bake in an oven preheated to 190°C/375°F/ Gas Mark 5 for 25–30 minutes until just cooked though.

3 Meanwhile, heat the remaining oil and fry the garlic, galangal and chillies for 30 seconds. Add the pepper and stir-fry for a further 2–3 minutes to soften.

4 Stir in the sugar, rice vinegar and water or fish stock, then add the tomatoes and bring to the boil. Remove the pan from the heat.

5 Remove the fish from the oven and transfer to a warmed serving plate. Add the fish juices to the pan, then spoon the sauce over the fish and scatter with the reserved basil leaves. Serve immediately.

COOK'S TIP

Large red chillies are less hot than the tiny red bird-eye chillies, so you can use them more freely in cooked dishes such as this for a mild heat. Remove the seeds if you prefer.

Chinese Whole Fried Fish

This impressive dish is worth cooking for a special dinner, as it really is a talking point. Buy a very fresh whole fish on the day you plan to cook it.

NUTRITIONAL INFORMATION

Calories 290	Sugars 7g
Protein 27g	Fat 11g
Carbohydrate . . .23g	Saturates 1g

🕭 🕭

🥗 30 mins   🕐 10 mins

SERVES 4–6

I N G R E D I E N T S

6 dried Chinese mushrooms

3 tbsp rice vinegar

2 tbsp soft light brown sugar

3 tbsp dark soy sauce

7.5 cm/3 inch piece fresh ginger root, finely chopped

4 spring onions, sliced diagonally

2 tsp cornflour

2 tbsp lime juice

1 sea bass, about 1 kg/2 lb 4 oz, cleaned

4 tbsp plain flour

sunflower oil for deep frying

salt and pepper

shredded Chinese leaves and radish slices, to serve

1 radish, sliced but left whole, to garnish

1 Soak the dried mushrooms in hot water for about 10 minutes, then drain, reserving 100 ml/3½ fl oz of the liquid. Cut the mushrooms into thin slices.

2 Put the reserved mushroom liquid in a saucepan with the rice vinegar, sugar, soy sauce, and mushrooms and bring to the boil. Simmer for 3–4 minutes.

3 Add the ginger and spring onions and simmer for 1 minute. Blend the cornflour and lime juice together, stir into the pan and stir for 1–2 minutes until the sauce thickens and clears. Keep to one side.

4 Season the fish inside and out with salt and pepper, then dust lightly with flour.

5 Heat a 2.5 cm/1 inch depth of oil in a wide, deep pan to 190°C/ 375°F. Carefully lower the fish into the oil and fry on one side for about 3–4 minutes until golden. Use 2 metal spatulas to turn the fish and fry on the other side for a further 3–4 minutes until golden brown.

6 Drain the fish. Serve with shredded Chinese leaves and radish slices, topped with the reheated sauce and garnished with the prepared radish.

Thai-spiced Salmon

Marinated in delicate Thai spices and quickly pan-fried to perfection, these salmon fillets are ideal for a special dinner.

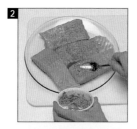

NUTRITIONAL INFORMATION

Calories 329	Sugars 0.1g	
Protein 30g	Fat 23g	
Carbohydrate . . .0.1g	Saturates 4g	

5 mins, plus 30 mins chilling   5 mins

SERVES 4

I N G R E D I E N T S

2.5 cm/1 in piece fresh root ginger, grated

1 tsp coriander seeds, crushed

¼ tsp chilli powder

1 tbsp lime juice

1 tsp sesame oil

4 pieces salmon fillet with skin, about 150 g/5½ oz each

2 tbsp vegetable oil

boiled rice and stir-fried vegetables

1 In a small bowl, mix together the grated fresh root ginger, crushed coriander, chilli powder, lime juice and sesame oil to make a marinade.

2 Place the salmon fillets side by side on a wide, non-metallic plate or dish and spoon the spice mixture over the flesh side of the fillets, spreading it so that it coats each piece of salmon evenly.

3 Cover the dish with cling film and chill the salmon in the refrigerator for at least 30 minutes.

4 Heat a wide, heavy-based frying pan or griddle pan with the vegetable oil over a high heat. Place the salmon on the hot pan or griddle, skin side down.

5 Cook the salmon for 4–5 minutes, without turning, until the salmon is crusty underneath and the flesh flakes easily. Serve at once with the boiled rice and stir-fried vegetables.

COOK'S TIP

It's important to use a heavy-based pan or solid griddle for this recipe, so the fish cooks evenly throughout without sticking. If the fish is very thick, you may prefer to turn it over carefully to cook on the other side for 2–3 minutes.

Spicy Thai Seafood Stew

This luxurious and deliciously fragrant Thai stew combines mixed seafood with spicy coconut sauce to make a mild curry.

NUTRITIONAL INFORMATION

Calories	288	Sugars	.........7g
Protein	........46g	Fat	..........8g
Carbohydrate	...10g	Saturates	.......1g

🥩 🥩

🍲 20 mins   🕐 5 mins

SERVES 4

I N G R E D I E N T S

200 g/7 oz squid, cleaned

500 g/1 lb 2 oz firm white fish fillet, preferably monkfish or halibut

1 tbsp sunflower oil

4 shallots, finely chopped

2 garlic cloves, finely chopped

2 tbsp green Thai curry paste

2 small lemon grass stalks, finely chopped

1 tsp shrimp paste

500 ml/18 fl oz coconut milk

200 g/7 oz raw tiger prawns, peeled, deveined

12 fresh clams in shells, cleaned

8 basil leaves, finely shredded

extra basil leaves, to garnish

boiled rice, to serve

1 Cut the squid body cavities into thick rings, and the firm, white fish into bite-sized chunks.

2 Heat the oil in a large frying pan or wok and stir-fry the shallots, garlic and curry paste for 1–2 minutes. Add the lemon grass and shrimp paste, stir in the coconut milk and bring to the boil. Reduce the heat until the liquid is simmering gently.

3 Add the prepared white fish, squid and prawns to the pan and simmer very gently for 2 minutes.

4 Add the clams and simmer for a further minute until the clams open. Discard any clams that do not open.

5 Scatter the shredded basil leaves over the stew, and serve immediately, with boiled rice, garnished with basil leaves.

COOK'S TIP

If you prefer, fresh mussels in shells can be used instead of clams. The white fish can be varied according to availability but should stay firm when cooked.

Spicy Scallops with Lime

Really fresh scallops have a delicate flavour and texture, needing only minimal cooking, as in this simple stir-fry.

NUTRITIONAL INFORMATION

Calories	145	Sugars	.........1g
Protein	........17g	Fat	...........7g
Carbohydrate	....4g	Saturates	.......3g

10 mins   8 mins

SERVES 4

I N G R E D I E N T S

16 large scallops

15 g/½ oz butter

1 tbsp vegetable oil

1 tsp garlic, crushed

1 tsp grated fresh ginger root

1 bunch spring onions,
    finely sliced

rind of 1 kaffir lime, finely grated

1 small red chilli, deseeded and very
    finely chopped

3 tbsp kaffir lime juice

salt and pepper

lime wedges and boiled rice, to serve

1 Trim the scallops to remove any black intestine, then wash and pat dry. Separate the corals from the white parts, then slice each white part into 2 rounds.

2 Heat the butter and oil in a frying pan or wok. Add the garlic and ginger and stir-fry for 1 minute without browning. Add the spring onions and continue to stir-fry for a minute.

3 Add the scallops and stir-fry over a high heat for 4–5 minutes. Stir in the lime rind, chilli and lime juice and cook for a minute more.

4 Serve the scallops hot, with the juices spooned over them, accompanied by lime wedges and boiled rice.

COOK'S TIP

If fresh scallops are not available, frozen ones can be used, but make sure they are thoroughly defrosted before you cook them. Drain off all the excess moisture and pat dry thoroughly with paper towels.

Prawn Skewers with Chilli

Whole tiger prawns cook very quickly on a barbecue or under a grill, so they are ideal for summertime cooking, in or out of doors.

NUTRITIONAL INFORMATION

Calories 106	Sugars 8g
Protein 11g	Fat 3g
Carbohydrate 8g	Saturates 1g

5 mins, plus 2 hrs marinating   6 mins

SERVES 4

INGREDIENTS

1 garlic clove, chopped

1 red bird-eye chilli, deseeded and chopped

1 tbsp tamarind paste

1 tbsp sesame oil

1 tbsp dark soy sauce

2 tbsp lime juice

1 tbsp soft light brown sugar

16 large whole raw tiger prawns

crusty bread, lime wedges and salad leaves, to serve

1 Put the garlic, chilli, tamarind paste, sesame oil, soy sauce, lime juice and sugar in a small saucepan. Stir over a low heat until the sugar has dissolved, then remove from the heat and allow to cool.

2 Wash and dry the prawns and place in a single layer in a wide, non-metallic dish. Spoon the marinade over the prawns and turn them over to coat evenly. Cover the dish and leave in the refrigerator to marinate for at least 2 hours, or preferably overnight.

3 When you are almost ready to cook the prawns, soak 4 bamboo or wooden skewers in water for about 20 minutes. Drain and thread 4 tiger prawns onto each skewer.

4 Grill the skewers under a preheated hot grill for 5–6 minutes, turning them over once, until they turn pink and begin to brown. Alternatively, barbecue over hot coals.

5 Thread a wedge of lime onto the end of each skewer and serve with crusty bread and salad leaves.

Thai Green Fish Curry

The pale green curry paste used in this recipe serves as the basis for a range of Thai dishes. It is delicious with chicken and beef, as well as fish.

NUTRITIONAL INFORMATION

Calories . . . . .217 Sugars 3g
Protein . . . . .12g Fat 17g
Carbohydrate . . . .5g Saturates 10g

15 mins   12 mins

SERVES 4

I N G R E D I E N T S

2 tbsp vegetable oil

1 garlic clove, chopped

1 small aubergine, diced

120 ml/4 fl oz coconut cream

2 tbsp Thai fish sauce

1 tsp sugar

225 g/8 oz firm white fish such as cod,
    haddock, halibut, cut into pieces

120 ml/4 fl oz fish stock

2 lime leaves, finely shredded

about 15 leaves Thai basil, if available,
    or ordinary basil

plain boiled rice or noodles, to serve

GREEN CURRY PASTE

5 fresh green chillies, deseeded
    and chopped

2 tsp chopped lemon grass

1 large shallot, chopped

2 garlic cloves, chopped

1 tsp freshly grated ginger or galangal

2 coriander roots, chopped

½ tsp ground coriander

¼ tsp ground cumin

1 kaffir lime leaf, finely chopped

1 tsp shrimp paste (optional)

½ tsp salt

1 Make the curry paste. Put all the ingredients into a blender or spice grinder and blend to a smooth paste, adding a little water if necessary.

2 In a frying pan or wok, heat the oil until almost smoking and add the garlic. Fry until golden. Add the curry paste and stir-fry a few seconds before adding the aubergine. Stir-fry for 4–5 minutes.

3 Add the coconut cream. Bring to the boil and stir until the cream thickens. Add the fish sauce and sugar.

4 Add the fish and stock. Simmer for 3–4 minutes, stirring occasionally, until the fish is just tender but still firm. Add the lime leaves and basil, and then cook for a further minute. Serve immediately with rice or noodles.

Mackerel Escabeche

Although the word *escabeche* – meaning pickled in vinegar – is Spanish in origin, variations of this dish are cooked all over the Mediterranean.

NUTRITIONAL INFORMATION

Calories 750	Sugars 3g
Protein 33g	Fat 63g
Carbohydrate ...12g	Saturates 11g

10 mins, plus 8 hrs cooling | 10 mins

SERVES 4

INGREDIENTS

150 ml/5 fl oz olive oil

4 mackerel, filleted

2 tbsp flour seasoned with salt and pepper, for dusting

4 tbsp red wine vinegar

1 onion, finely sliced

1 strip orange rind, removed with a potato peeler

1 sprig fresh thyme

1 sprig fresh rosemary

1 fresh bay leaf

4 garlic cloves, crushed

2 fresh red chillies, bruised

1 tsp salt

3 tbsp chopped fresh flat-leaf parsley

1 Heat half the oil in a frying pan and dust the mackerel fillets with the seasoned flour. Shake off any excess.

2 Add the fish to the frying pan and cook for about 30 seconds on each side. (This does not cook the fish through.)

3 Transfer the mackerel to a shallow dish which is large enough to hold the fillets in one layer.

4 Place the the vinegar, onion, orange rind, thyme, rosemary, bay leaf, garlic, chillies and salt in the frying pan and heat the mixture slowly, then simmer it gently for about 10 minutes.

5 Add the remaining olive oil and the chopped parsley to the mixture, then pour it over the fish. Leave it to cool and when it is cold, serve the dish with plenty of crusty bread.

VARIATION

Substitute 12 whole sardines, cleaned, with heads removed. Cook in the same way. Tuna steaks are also delicious served escabeche.

Red Prawn Curry

Like all Thai curries, this one has as its base a hot paste of chillies and spices and a delicious sauce of coconut milk.

NUTRITIONAL INFORMATION

Calories	149	Sugars	.........4g
Protein	........15g	Fat	..........7g
Carbohydrate	....6g	Saturates	.......1g

10 mins   10 mins

SERVES 4

I N G R E D I E N T S

2 tbsp vegetable oil

1 garlic clove, finely chopped

1 tbsp red curry paste

200 ml/7 fl oz coconut milk

2 tbsp Thai fish sauce

1 tsp sugar

12 large raw prawns, deveined

2 lime leaves, finely shredded

1 small red chilli, deseeded and finely sliced

10 leaves Thai basil, if available,
   or ordinary basil

RED CURRY PASTE

3 dried long red chillies

½ tsp ground coriander

¼ tsp ground cumin

½ tsp ground black pepper

2 garlic cloves, chopped

2 stalks lemon grass, chopped

1 kaffir lime leaf, finely chopped

1 tsp freshly grated root ginger or
   galangal, if available

1 tsp shrimp paste (optional)

½ tsp salt

1 Make the red curry paste. Put all the ingredients in a blender or spice grinder and blend to a smooth paste, adding a little water if necessary. Alternatively, pound the ingredients using a mortar and pestle until smooth.

2 Heat the oil in a wok or frying pan until almost smoking. Add the garlic and fry until golden. Add 1 tablespoon of the curry paste and cook for 1 minute.

Add half the coconut milk, the fish sauce and sugar. The mixture will thicken slightly.

3 Add the prawns and simmer for 3–4 minutes until they turn colour. Add the remaining coconut milk, the lime leaves and the chilli. Cook for 2–3 minutes until the prawns are just tender.

4 Add the basil leaves, stir until wilted and serve immediately.

Prawns with Courgettes

This curry will be very quick to cook if you have prepared the ingredients beforehand – including measuring out the spices.

NUTRITIONAL INFORMATION

Calories 272   Sugars 5g
Protein . . . . .29g   Fat 15g
Carbohydrate . . . .5g   Saturates 2g

10 mins, plus 30 mins standing   10 mins

SERVES 4

INGREDIENTS

350 g/12 oz small courgettes

1 tsp salt

450 g/1 lb cooked tiger prawns

5 tbsp vegetable oil

4 garlic cloves, finely chopped

5 tbsp chopped fresh coriander

1 fresh green chilli, deseeded and finely chopped

½ tsp ground turmeric

1½ tsp ground cumin

pinch cayenne pepper

200 g/7 oz canned chopped tomatoes

1 tsp freshly grated ginger

1 tbsp lemon juice

steamed basmati rice, to serve

1 Cut the courgettes into batons. Put into a colander and sprinkle with a little of the salt. Set aside for 30 minutes. Rinse, drain and pat dry. Spread the prawns on paper towels to drain.

2 In a wok or frying pan, heat the oil over a high heat. Add the garlic. As soon as it begins to brown, add the courgettes, coriander, green chilli, turmeric, cumin, cayenne, tomatoes, ginger, lemon juice and remaining salt. Stir well and bring to the boil.

3 Cover the pan and simmer over a low heat for about 5 minutes. Uncover and add the prawns.

4 Increase the heat to high and simmer for about 5 minutes to reduce the liquid to a thick sauce. Serve immediately with steamed basmati rice, generously garnished with lime wedges.

VARIATION
If you can't find cooked tiger prawns for this recipe, use cooked peeled small prawns instead, but these release quite a lot of liquid so you may need to increase the final simmering time to thicken the sauce.

Mackerel with Lime

The secret of this barbecued dish lies in the simple, fresh flavours of coriander and lime which perfectly complement the fish.

NUTRITIONAL INFORMATION

Calories 302	Sugars 0g	
Protein 21g	Fat 24g	
Carbohydrate 0g	Saturates 4g	

   10 mins   🕐 10 mins

SERVES 4

INGREDIENTS

4 small mackerel

¼ tsp ground coriander

¼ tsp ground cumin

4 sprigs fresh coriander

3 tbsp chopped, fresh coriander

1 red chilli, deseeded and chopped

grated rind and juice of 1 lime

2 tbsp sunflower oil

salt and pepper

1 lime, sliced, to garnish

chilli flowers (optional), to garnish

salad leaves, to serve

1 To make the chilli flowers (if using), cut the tip of a small chilli lengthways into thin strips, leaving the chilli intact at the stem end. Remove the seeds and place in iced water until curled.

2 Clean and gut the mackerel, removing the heads if preferred. Transfer the mackerel to a chopping board.

COOK'S TIP

This recipe is suitable for other oily fish, such as trout, herring and sardines. Ask the fishmonger to gut the fish for you, if you prefer.

3 Sprinkle the fish inside and outside with the ground coriander and cumin and salt and pepper to taste. Sprinkle 1 teaspoon of the chopped coriander inside the cavity of each fish.

4 Place the remaining chopped coriander, chilli, lime rind and juice and the sunflower oil in a small bowl and mix thoroughly. Brush the mixture liberally over both sides of the fish.

5 Place the fish in a hinged rack if you have one. Barbecue the fish over hot coals for 3–4 minutes on each side, turning once. Brush the fish frequently with the remaining basting mixture. Transfer to plates and garnish with chilli flowers (if using) and lime slices, and serve with salad.

Szechuan White Fish

Szechuan pepper is not related to ordinary black pepper, but is the dried berry of a shrub in the citrus family. It should be used sparingly.

NUTRITIONAL INFORMATION

Calories	225	Sugars	.........3g
Protein	........20g	Fat	...........8g
Carbohydrate	...17g	Saturates	.......1g

🍖 🍖 🍖

🥘 10 mins   🕐 15 mins

SERVES 4

INGREDIENTS

350 g/12 oz white fish fillets

1 small egg, beaten

3 tbsp plain flour

4 tbsp dry white wine

3 tbsp light soy sauce

vegetable oil, for deep-frying

1 garlic clove, cut into slivers

1 cm/½ inch piece fresh root ginger, finely chopped

1 onion, finely chopped

1 celery stick, chopped

1 fresh red chilli, chopped

3 spring onions, chopped

1 tsp rice wine vinegar

½ tsp ground Szechuan pepper

175 ml/6 fl oz fish stock

1 tsp caster sugar

1 tsp cornflour

2 tsp water

1 Cut the fish into 4 cm/1½ inch cubes. Beat together the egg, flour, wine and 1 tablespoon of soy sauce to make a batter. Dip the cubes of fish into the batter to coat well.

2 Heat the oil in a wok, reduce the heat slightly and cook the fish in batches, for 2–3 minutes, until golden brown. Remove with a slotted spoon, drain on kitchen paper, set aside and keep warm.

3 Cool the oil, then pour all but about 1 tablespoon from the wok and return to the heat. Add the garlic, ginger, onion, celery, chilli and spring onions and stir-fry for 1–2 minutes. Stir in the remaining soy sauce and the vinegar.

4 Add the Szechuan pepper, fish stock and sugar. Mix the cornflour with the water to form a smooth paste and stir it into the stock. Bring to the boil and cook, stirring, for 1 minute, until the sauce thickens and clears.

5 Return the fish cubes to the wok and cook for 1–2 minutes to heat through. Serve immediately.

Indonesian-style Spicy Cod

A delicious aromatic coating of coconut and spices makes this dish rather special. Serve it with a crisp salad and crusty bread.

NUTRITIONAL INFORMATION

Calories	146	Sugars	........2g
Protein	........19g	Fat	..........7g
Carbohydrate	....2g	Saturates	......4g

10 mins   15 mins

SERVES 4

INGREDIENTS

4 cod steaks

1 stalk lemon grass

1 small red onion, chopped

3 cloves garlic, chopped

2 fresh red chillies, deseeded and chopped

1 tsp grated fresh root ginger

¼ tsp turmeric

2 tbsp butter, cut into small cubes

8 tbsp coconut milk

2 tbsp lemon juice

salt and pepper

red chillies, to garnish (optional)

1 Rinse the cod steaks and pat them dry on absorbent kitchen paper.

2 Remove and discard the outer leaves from the lemon grass and thinly slice the inner section.

3 Place the lemon grass, onion, garlic, chillies, root ginger and turmeric in a food processor and blend just until the ingredients are finely chopped. Season with salt and pepper to taste.

4 With the processor running, add the butter, coconut milk and lemon juice and process until well blended.

5 Place the fish in a shallow, non-metallic dish. Pour the coconut mixture over it and turn the fish to coat it.

6 If you have one, place the fish steaks in a hinged basket. Barbecue over hot coals for 15 minutes or until the fish is cooked through, turning once. Serve garnished with red chillies (if using).

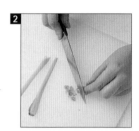

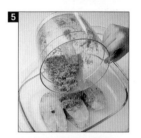

COOK'S TIP

If you prefer a milder flavour, omit the chillies altogether. For a hotter flavour do not remove the seeds from one or both of the chillies.

Hot & Sour Beef Salad

Thais are primarily fish-eaters, so beef usually only appears on the menu for feast days. But, as in this dish, a little can go a long way.

NUTRITIONAL INFORMATION

Calories 207	Sugars 7g	
Protein 15g	Fat 13g	
Carbohydrate 9g	Saturates 3g	

15 mins   4 mins

SERVES 4

INGREDIENTS

1 tsp black peppercorns

1 tsp coriander seeds

1 dried red bird-eye chilli

¼ tsp five-spice powder

250 g/9 oz beef fillet

1 tbsp dark soy sauce

6 spring onions

1 carrot

¼ cucumber

8 radishes

1 red onion

¼ head Chinese leaves

2 tbsp groundnut oil

1 garlic clove, crushed

1 tsp finely chopped lemon grass

1 tbsp chopped fresh mint

1 tbsp chopped fresh coriander

DRESSING

3 tbsp lime juice

1 tbsp light soy sauce

2 tsp soft light brown sugar

1 tsp sesame oil

1 Crush the peppercorns, coriander seeds and chilli in a pestle and mortar, then mix with the five-spice powder and sprinkle on a plate. Brush the beef all over with soy sauce, then roll it in the spices to coat evenly.

2 Cut the spring onions into 6 cm/2½ inch lengths and then shred them finely lengthways. Place in iced water and leave until curled. Drain well.

3 Trim the carrot and cut into very thin diagonal slices. Halve the cucumber and scoop out the seeds, then slice thinly. Trim the radishes and cut into flower shapes.

4 Cut the onion into thin, vertical slices. Roughly shred the Chinese leaves. Toss all the vegetables together in a large salad bowl.

5 Heat the oil in a heavy-based frying pan and fry the garlic and lemon grass until just turning golden brown. Add the steak and press down with a spatula to ensure it browns evenly. Cook for 3–4 minutes, turning it over once. Remove the pan from the heat.

6 Slice the steak thinly and toss into the salad with the mint and coriander. Mix together the dressing ingredients, stir into the pan, then spoon over the salad.

Papaya & Avocado Salad

This colourful and refreshing salad, with its sweet and spicy flavours, is the perfect foil to a meaty main dish.

NUTRITIONAL INFORMATION

Calories 194   Sugars 7g
Protein . . . . .4g   Fat 16g
Carbohydrate . . . .9g   Saturates 3g

 10 mins   0 mins

SERVES 4–6

INGREDIENTS

200 g/7 oz mixed green salad leaves

2–3 spring onions, chopped

3–4 tbsp chopped fresh coriander

1 small papaya

2 red peppers

1 avocado

1 tbsp lime juice

3–4 tbsp pumpkin seeds, preferably toasted (optional)

DRESSING

juice of 1 lime

large pinch of paprika

large pinch of ground cumin

large pinch of sugar

1 garlic clove, finely chopped

4 tbsp extra-virgin olive oil

dash of white wine vinegar (optional)

salt

1 Combine the salad leaves with the spring onions and coriander. Toss together, then transfer the salad to a large serving dish.

2 Cut the papaya in half and scoop out the seeds with a spoon. Cut into quarters, remove the peel and slice the flesh. Arrange on top of the salad leaves.

Cut the peppers in half, remove the cores and seeds, then slice thinly. Add the peppers to the salad leaves.

3 Cut the avocado in half around the stone. Twist apart, then remove the stone with a knife. Carefully peel off the skin, dice the flesh and toss in lime juice to prevent the avocado from discolouring. Add to the other salad ingredients.

4 To make the dressing, whisk together the lime juice, paprika, ground cumin, sugar, garlic and olive oil. Add salt if desired, to suit your taste.

5 Pour the dressing over the salad and toss lightly, adding a dash of wine vinegar if a flavour with more 'bite' is preferred. Sprinkle with the toasted pumpkin seeds, if using.

Mexican Potato Salad

This dish is full of enticing Mexican flavours. Potato slices are topped with tomatoes, chillies and peppers, and served with a guacamole dressing.

NUTRITIONAL INFORMATION

Calories 260	Sugars 6g
Protein 6g	Fat 9g
Carbohydrate . . .41g	Saturates 2g

10 mins, plus cooling

15 mins

SERVES 4

INGREDIENTS

4 large waxy potatoes, sliced

1 ripe avocado

1 tsp olive oil

1 tsp lemon juice

1 garlic clove, crushed

1 onion, chopped

2 large tomatoes, sliced

1 green chilli, chopped

1 yellow pepper, sliced

2 tbsp chopped fresh coriander

salt and pepper

lemon wedges, to garnish

1 Cook the potato slices in a saucepan of boiling water for 10-15 minutes or until tender. Drain and leave to cool.

2 Meanwhile, cut the avocado in half and remove the stone. Using a spoon, scoop the avocado flesh from the 2 halves and place in a mixing bowl.

3 Mash the avocado flesh with a fork and stir in the olive oil, lemon juice, garlic and chopped onion. Cover the bowl and set aside.

4 Mix the tomatoes, chilli and yellow pepper together and transfer to a salad bowl with the potato slices.

5 Spoon the avocado mixture on top and sprinkle with the coriander. Season to taste and serve garnished with lemon wedges.

COOK'S TIP

Choose a ripe avocado that yields to gentle pressure from your thumb. Mixing the avocado flesh with lemon juice prevents it from turning brown once exposed to the air.

Potato & Chicken Salad

The spicy peanut dressing served with this salad may be prepared in advance and left to chill a day before required.

NUTRITIONAL INFORMATION

Calories	802	Sugars	......15g
Protein	......35g	Fat	........55g
Carbohydrate	...45g	Saturates	.....10g

 10 mins   10 mins

SERVES 4

INGREDIENTS

4 large waxy potatoes

300 g/10½ oz fresh pineapple, diced

2 carrots, grated

175 g/6 oz bean sprouts

1 bunch spring onions, sliced

1 large courgette, cut into matchsticks

3 celery sticks, cut into matchsticks

175 g/6 oz unsalted peanuts

2 cooked chicken breast fillets, about 125 g/4½ oz each, sliced

DRESSING

6 tbsp crunchy peanut butter

6 tbsp olive oil

2 tbsp light soy sauce

1 red chilli, chopped

2 tsp sesame oil

4 tsp lime juice

1 Cut the potatoes into small dice and cook in a saucepan of boiling water, for 10 minutes or until just tender. Drain and leave to cool, then transfer to a large salad bowl.

2 Add the pineapple, carrots, bean sprouts, spring onions, courgette, celery, peanuts and sliced chicken to the potatoes. Toss well.

3 To make the dressing, put the peanut butter in a small mixing bowl and gradually whisk in the olive oil and light soy sauce. Stir in the chopped red chilli, sesame oil and lime juice. Mix until well combined.

4 Pour the spicy dressing over the salad and toss lightly to coat all of the ingredients. Serve immediately.

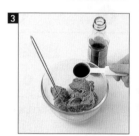

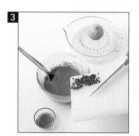

COOK'S TIP

Unsweetened canned pineapple may be used in place of the fresh pineapple for convenience. If only sweetened canned pineapple is available, drain it and rinse under cold running water before using.

Gingered Potatoes

This is a simple spicy dish which is ideal with a plain main course.
The cashew nuts and celery add extra crunch.

NUTRITIONAL INFORMATION

Calories ...... .325   Sugars 1g
Protein .... .5g   Fat .... .21g
Carbohydrate ...30g   Saturates 9g

 10 mins   🕐 25 mins

SERVES 4

I N G R E D I E N T S

675 g/1½ lb waxy potatoes, cut into
  chunky pieces

few strands of saffron

2 tbsp vegetable oil

5 cm/2 inch piece of root ginger, grated

1 green chilli, chopped

1 celery stick, chopped

25 g/1 oz cashew nuts

3 tbsp boiling water

60 g/2 oz butter

celery leaves, to garnish

1 Cook the potatoes in a saucepan of boiling water for 10 minutes, then drain thoroughly.

2 Place the saffron strands in a small bowl. Add the boiling water and set aside to soak for 5 minutes.

3 Heat the oil in a heavy-based frying pan and add the potatoes. Cook over a medium heat, stirring constantly to prevent sticking, for 3-4 minutes.

4 Add the grated ginger, chilli, celery and cashew nuts and cook for 1 minute.

5 Add the butter to the pan, lower the heat and stir in the saffron mixture. Cook over a low heat for 10 minutes, or until the potatoes are tender.

6 Transfer to a warm serving dish, garnish the gingered potatoes with the celery leaves and serve at once.

COOK'S TIP

Use a non-stick, heavy-based frying
pan as the potato mixture is fairly dry
and may stick to an ordinary pan.

Courgette & Tomato Salad

Lightly cooked courgettes are mixed with ripe, juicy tomatoes and dressed with a chilli vinaigrette to create a perfect side salad.

NUTRITIONAL INFORMATION

Calories	92	Sugars	.........3g
Protein	.........2g	Fat	...........8g
Carbohydrate	....4g	Saturates	.......1g

🥘 🥘

10 mins, plus 20 mins standing   🕐 20 mins

SERVES 4–6

I N G R E D I E N T S

1 large fresh mild green chilli, or a combination of 1 green pepper and ½–1 fresh green chilli

4 courgettes, sliced

2–3 garlic cloves, finely chopped

pinch sugar

¼ tsp ground cumin

2 tbsp white wine vinegar

4 tbsp extra-virgin olive oil

2–3 tbsp coriander

4 ripe tomatoes, diced or sliced

salt and pepper

1 Roast the mild chilli, or the combination of the green pepper and chilli, in a heavy-based ungreased frying pan or under a preheated grill until the skin is charred. Place in a plastic bag, twist to seal well and leave the mixture to stand for 20 minutes.

2 Peel the skin from the chilli and pepper, if using, then carefully remove the core and seeds and slice the flesh. Set aside.

3 Bring about 5 cm/2 inches water to the boil in the bottom of a steamer. Add the courgettes to the top part of the steamer, cover with a lid and steam for about 5 minutes until just tender.

4 Meanwhile, combine the garlic, sugar, cumin, vinegar, olive oil and coriander thoroughly in a bowl. Stir in the chilli and pepper, if you are using it, then season with salt and pepper to taste.

5 Arrange the courgettes and tomatoes in a serving bowl or on a platter and spoon over the chilli dressing. Serve the salad immediately.

VARIATION

Add 225 g/8oz cooked peeled prawns to the courgettes and tomatoes, before coating with the dressing.

Spicy Cauliflower

This is a perfectly delicious way to serve cauliflower. It can be enjoyed as a salad or at a picnic, or as a side dish to a main meal.

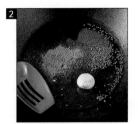
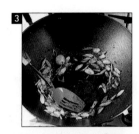

NUTRITIONAL INFORMATION

Calories	68	Sugars	....3g
Protein	....5g	Fat	....4g
Carbohydrate	....4g	Saturates	....1g

 5 mins   15 mins

SERVES 4

I N G R E D I E N T S

500 g/1 lb 2 oz cauliflower, cut into florets

1 tbsp sunflower oil

1 garlic clove

½ tsp turmeric

1 tsp cumin seeds, ground

1 tsp coriander seeds, ground

1 tsp yellow mustard seeds

12 spring onions, sliced finely

salt and pepper

1 Cook the cauliflower lightly in boiling water, drain, and set aside.

2 Heat the oil gently in a large, heavy frying pan or wok. Add the whole garlic clove, turmeric, ground cumin, ground coriander and mustard seeds. Stir well and cover the pan.

3 When the mustard seeds start to pop, add the spring onions and stir. Cook for 2 minutes, stirring constantly, to soften them a little. Season to taste.

4 Add the cauliflower and stir for 3–4 minutes until coated completely with the spices and thoroughly heated.

5 Remove the garlic clove. Transfer the cauliflower to a serving dish and serve immediately, while still hot.

COOK'S TIP

For a special occasion this dish looks great made with baby cauliflowers instead of florets. Peel off most of the outer leaves, leaving a few for decoration, blanch the cauliflowers whole for 4 minutes and drain. Continue as in step 2.

Exotic Fruit Salad

This colourful fruit salad, infused with the delicate flavours of jasmine tea and ginger, makes an exotic, light dessert.

NUTRITIONAL INFORMATION

Calories ....65 Sugars 16g
Protein ....1g Fat 0g
Carbohydrate ...16g Saturates 0g

15 mins, plus
1 hr chilling

0 mins

SERVES 6

INGREDIENTS

1 tsp jasmine tea

1 tsp grated fresh ginger root

1 strip lime rind

120 ml/4 fl oz boiling water

2 tbsp caster sugar

1 papaya

1 mango

½ small pineapple

1 starfruit

2 passion fruit

juice of ½–1 lime

1 Place the tea, ginger and lime rind in a heatproof jug and pour over the boiling water. Leave to infuse for 5 minutes, then strain the liquid.

2 Add the sugar to the liquid and stir well to dissolve. Leave the syrup until it is completely cool.

3 Halve, deseed and peel the papaya. Halve the mango, remove the stone and peel. Peel and remove the core from the pineapple. Cut the fruits into bite-sized pieces.

4 Slice the starfruit crossways. Place all the prepared fruits in a wide serving bowl and pour over the cooled syrup. Cover with cling film and chill for about 1 hour.

5 Cut the passion-fruit in half, scoop out the flesh and mix it with the lime juice. Spoon over the prepared salad and serve immediately.

COOK'S TIP

Starfruit have little flavour when unripe and green, but once ripened and turned yellow they become delicately sweet and fragrant. Usually by this stage, the tips of the ridges have become brown, so you will need to remove these before slicing.

Lychee & Ginger Sorbet

A refreshing palate-cleanser after a rich meal, this quick and simple sorbet can be served alone or with fruit salad.

NUTRITIONAL INFORMATION

Calories 159	Sugars 40g
Protein 2g	Fat 0g
Carbohydrate ...40g	Saturates 0g

5 mins, plus 5–6 hrs freezing   0 mins

SERVES 4

I N G R E D I E N T S

2 T 400 g/14 oz cans lychees in syrup

rind of 1 lime, finely grated

2 tbsp lime juice

3 tbsp stem ginger syrup

2 egg whites

T O   D E C O R A T E

starfruit slices

slivers of stem ginger

1 Drain the lychees, reserving the syrup. Place the fruits in a blender or food processor with the lime rind, juice and stem ginger syrup and process until completely smooth. Transfer to a mixing bowl.

2 Mix the purée thoroughly with the reserved lychee syrup, then pour into a freezerproof container and freeze for 1–1½ hours until slushy in texture. (Alternatively, use an ice-cream maker.)

3 Remove from the freezer and whisk to break up the ice crystals. Whisk the egg whites in a clean, dry bowl with a clean whisk until stiff, then quickly and lightly fold into the iced mixture.

4 Return to the freezer and freeze until firm. Serve the sorbet in scoops decorated with starfruit and ginger.

COOK'S TIP

It is not recommended that raw egg whites are served to very young children, pregnant women, the elderly or anyone weakened by chronic illness.

Steamed Coconut Cake

This steamed coconut cake, steeped in a syrup of lime and ginger, is typical of Thai desserts and sweets. It has a distinctly Chinese influence.

NUTRITIONAL INFORMATION

Calories	243	Sugars	........17g
Protein	.........4g	Fat	..........12g
Carbohydrate	...31g	Saturates	.......8g

 15 mins 30 mins

SERVES 8

I N G R E D I E N T S

2 large eggs, separated

pinch of salt

100 g/3½ oz caster sugar

75 g/2¾ oz/5 tbsp butter, melted and cooled

5 tbsp coconut milk

150 g/5½ oz self-raising flour

½ tsp baking powder

3 tbsp desiccated coconut

4 tbsp stem ginger syrup

3 tbsp lime juice

TO DECORATE

3 pieces stem ginger, diced

curls of freshly grated coconut

strips of lime rind

1 Cut a 28 cm/11 inch round of non-stick paper and press into an 18 cm/ 7 inch steamer basket to line it.

COOK'S TIP

Coconuts grow on tropical beaches all around the world, but probably originated in South-East Asia, and it is here that coconut is most important in cooking.

2 Whisk the egg whites with the salt until stiff. Gradually whisk in the sugar, 1 tablespoon at a time, whisking hard after each addition until the mixture stands in stiff peaks.

3 Whisk in the yolks, then quickly stir in the butter and coconut milk. Sift the flour and baking powder over the mixture, then fold in lightly and evenly with a large metal spoon. Fold in the coconut.

4 Spoon the mixture into the lined steamer basket and tuck the spare paper over the top. Place the basket over boiling water, cover and steam for 30 minutes.

5 Turn the cake onto a plate, remove the paper and cool slightly. Mix together the ginger syrup and lime juice and spoon over the cake. Cut into squares and top with ginger, coconut and lime rind.

Melon & Ginger Crush

A really refreshing summer drink, this melon crush is quick and simple to make. If you can't buy kaffir limes, ordinary limes are fine.

NUTRITIONAL INFORMATION

Calories	46	Sugars	.........7g
Protein	.........1g	Fat	...........0g
Carbohydrate	....7g	Saturates	.......0g

  5 mins   0 mins

SERVES 4

I N G R E D I E N T S

1 melon, about 800 g/1 lb 12 oz

6 tbsp ginger wine

3 tbsp kaffir lime juice

ice, crushed

1 lime

1 Peel and deseed the melon and roughly chop the flesh. Place it in a blender or a food processor with the ginger wine and the lime juice.

2 Blend on high speed until the mixture is completely smooth.

3 Put plenty of crushed ice into 4 tall tumblers. Pour the melon and ginger crush over the ice.

4 Cut the lime into slim slices, cut a slit in each one and slip it onto the side of a glass. Serve immediately.

VARIATION

If you prefer a non-alcoholic version of this drink, simply omit the ginger wine, then top up with ginger ale in the glass. For a change of flavour, use a watermelon when they are in season. Ginger wine is available from wine shops.

NOTE

This book uses metric and imperial measurements. Follow the same units
of measurement throughout; do not mix metric and imperial.
All spoon measurements are level: teaspoons are assumed to be 5 ml, and
tablespoons are assumed to be 15 ml. Unless otherwise stated,
milk is assumed to be full fat, eggs and individual vegetables such as potatoes
are medium, and pepper is freshly ground black pepper.

The nutritional information provided for each recipe is per serving or per person.
Optional ingredients, variations or serving suggestions have
not been included in the calculations. The times given for each recipe are an approximate
guide only because the preparation times may differ according to the techniques used by
different people and the cooking times may vary as a result of the type of oven used.

Recipes using raw or very lightly cooked eggs should be
avoided by infants, the elderly, pregnant women, convalescents,
and anyone suffering from an illness.

*The publisher would like to thank
Steamer Trading Cookshop, Lewes, East Sussex, for the kind loan of props.*